THE STREETS CAN'T HAVE MY SON

OSCEOLA THOMAS, MS

SD

SOUND DOCTRINE PUBLISHING

SOUND DOCTRINE PUBLISHING

The Streets Can't Have My Son by Osceola Thomas

Copyright © 2015 by Osceola Thomas. All rights reserved.

No part of this book may be reproduced in any written, electronic, recording, or photocopying without written permission of the publisher or author. The exception would be in the case of brief quotations embodied in the critical articles or reviews and pages where permission is specifically granted by the publisher or author.

Although every precaution has been taken to verify the accuracy of the information contained herein, the author and publisher assume no responsibility for any errors or omissions. No liability is assumed for damages that may result from the use of information contained within.

Books may be purchased in quantity and/or special sales by contacting the publisher and author at:

Sound Doctrine Publishing Incorporated

Author page: www.thestreetscanthavemyson.com

By phone: 704-497-2332

Email: info@thestreetscanthavemyson.com.

ISBN-13: 978-0692383254

ISBN-10: 0692383255

1. Education 2. Black Studies

First Edition Printed in the United States of America

Dedication

This book is dedicated to all of the black sons who left us too soon.

Rest in peace.

Table of Contents

ACKNOWLEDGEMENTS vii
FOREWORD ix
PREFACE xi
THE NEW PLANTATION xvii

PART 1: THE MATTER AT HAND
KILLING THE DREAM 3
IDEA: INDIVIDUALS DESTROYING EDUCATIONAL
ASPIRATIONS 9
BLACK BOYS:
PUBLIC ENEMY NUMBER ONE 25

PART 2: WHAT TEACHERS AND ADMINISTRATORS CAN DO
DIFFERENTIATED INSTRUCTION DISORDER 41
DON'T MAKE ASSUMPTIONS 57
TRIBUTE TO HIP HOP 65
FOCUS ON THE STRENGTHS 67
WHERE IS MY FATHER? 81

PART 3: WHAT PARENTS CAN DO
KNOWLEDGE OF SELF 85
BESTOW THE BLESSING 91
WHAT DO WE DO? 99

PART 4: WHAT COMMUNITIES CAN DO
A SHARED VISION FOR CHANGE 103

SELECTED BIBLIOGRAPHY 115
INDEX 121
SUGGESTED READING LIST 123
ABOUT THE AUTHOR 125

Acknowledgements

I am indebted to a number of people who without their contributions this book would not have been possible: the late Mark Copeland, Aaron Means, Pastor Michael Coe, Colette Jeffries, Darrell Gregory, and Dr. Chance Lewis. I am truly grateful for your friendship and support.

I would also like to thank my mother Mary Thomas and brother Darrell Thomas for your unconditional love during my wayward years. You were there for me when I was at my lowest point. Thank you.

I am most appreciative to my wife and educator Kimberly for her commitment to children. You are what every educator should aspire to become.

Lastly, I want to especially thank my son and daughter Brandon and Lauren for being the kind of children that any father would be proud to acknowledge as his own. I love you very much!

Foreword

A critical and strategic examination of the social science and popular literature along with recent events across the United States highlight the complexities of being a Black male in today's society. The current trends surrounding academic achievement, incarceration rates, unemployment and underemployment along with a host of other issues disheartens me deeply because of the slow death of life opportunities for Black males that should be positioned to be our future leaders. As an educator, it further disheartens me to examine data from the National Assessment of Educational Progress, a division of the United States Department of Education, that highlights that over 70 percent of Black males have not reached basic proficiency levels in core academic subjects (math, science, English, social studies, etc.) at the middle and high school levels. This comes at a time when our nation has made increased financial and strategic investment in STEM (Science, Technology, Engineering and Mathematics) in secondary as well as postsecondary education to maintain our position as a world superpower. However, where are the benefits for Black males in this investment? We must ask the question, "Will this investment yield positive returns for Black males and their life opportunities?"

The Streets Can't Have My Son makes an important and much needed contribution to the national discourse on Black males in a time where the national trend in the Black community is that Black Lives Matter! Osceola Thomas has assembled a powerful set of chapters that reverse the tide of negativity towards Black males and move us closer to the Dream that Dr. Martin Luther King, Jr. envisioned. It is my hope that this book will bring this nation together to ask one fundamental question, 'What can I do to help?' Further, I hope everyone will now see the true value Black males bring to this great nation.

In closing, I commend Osceola Thomas for this book. These chapters bring thought-provoking and real world perspectives on the future of Black males in the United States. As a result, I will certainly add this book to my library.

Chance W. Lewis, Ph.D.

Carol Grotnes Belk Distinguished Professor of Urban Education

Director, The Urban Education Collaborative

College of Education

The University of North Carolina at Charlotte

Preface

The year is 1986, a 17-year-old African American male prepares to walk across the stage to receive his general equivalency diploma at a Youth Corp commencement ceremony. As the master of ceremony calls out his name, he makes his way toward the lectern to receive a piece of paper that would forever invalidate all of his future educational achievements. The experience, while a congratulatory one, is not able to combat his feelings of failure and inadequacy. He looks out into the audience at his mother and younger brother who despite his failure, manage to display looks of pride. It is at that very moment that reality sets in forcing him to acknowledge that he is a high school dropout.

While I am sure that my situation is not unique considering the disproportionate number of African American boys dropping out of high school each year. If I could go back in time and erase that moment in history, I surely would. Despite my having earned a Bachelor of Science and Master of Science degrees from a conservative evangelical institution, it has not been able to make up for the pain I feel for having deprived my parents the opportunity to see their eldest son graduate from high school. That is the main reason for me writing this book. I wanted to somehow play a part in helping to increase the number of Black males graduating from high school so they would not grow up feeling like I did because they failed to obtain a high school education.

Another reason forcing me to release this manuscript is in large part due to our current social climate and the unfair losses of youth like Michael Brown, Trayvon Martin, Jonathan Ferrell, and Oscar Grant. Surely, we lost these young men too soon. In each of these cases, institutional racism was the culprit and it has to be confronted and eradicated beginning with our most fundamental social institution: public education. The public school system, as this book will demonstrate, is killing the spirit and aspirations of Black boys more than any other institution in our country through their use of deficit-based labels, special education placements, and excessive discipline policies that result in their chronic absenteeism and future incarceration. This is deliberate and by design. America has painted Black boys as the poster child for unintelligence and delinquency to maintain her lower class and cheap prison workforce. And while my assessment may paint an extreme picture for a particular racial group, let me state for the record that I am not now nor have I ever been a racist. I am, however, a realist and right now in America we have a real problem.

The American public school system is graduating 59 percent of the black males in its classrooms. This means that if I graded America on her ability to prepare Black boys for post-secondary learning and high wage earning careers using her grading system, she would receive an "F" on her report card! Surely, the public school system has accomplished its objective of leaving Black boys behind. Of necessity, educational agencies must take a new approach at how they instruct Black boys and examine the root causes of academic failure for this particular group of students because in truth, Black Lives Do Matter.

Please understand that it is not my intent in writing this book to create an antagonistic relationship with the public school system. I am, however, seeking to draw attention to the disproportionality of Black boys in special education and youth correctional facilities. This issue has existed far too long and for many educators, the failure of Black boys has become the rule rather than the exception. What a sad commentary. Unlike many of my peers who write about the state of Black boys in public education, I am not a teacher by conventional standards. My professional credentials are not in early childhood education nor did I take the Praxis to be considered highly qualified. I rely solely on my experience working with public school systems and juvenile justice agencies throughout the country to establish me as a qualified individual to write on the state of Black males in America's classrooms and locked facilities.

As a Black male and advocate for youth, I am seriously concerned about White America's deliberate attempt to sabotage the future of Black boys. That racist policies, implicit biases, and a lack of resources are factors directly responsible for the disparities between Black boys and their White counterparts are issues that we cannot easily dismiss. Proposed in the upcoming chapters, are practical strategies for parents, teachers, and community groups to involve themselves in the educational process as well as alternatives to suspensions and court involvement in addressing the state of Black males.

This change must begin with the public school system and their deliberate mistreatment and mis-education of its Black male students. Alternatives to punitive strategies for this group of students along with a willingness to assess and plan for the non-academic barriers that are negatively impacting student learning must become a priority if schools expect to advance their Black male students. When administrators choose to suspend and arrest their Black boys for minor infractions, it not only removes them from the classroom resulting in loss of instructional days; it also contributes to their academic failure and dropping out of school. And what viable options does a high school dropout have? This provides us a direct correlation between school discipline policies and juvenile incarceration or the more popular catch phrase: "the school to prison pipeline." How unfortunate that school systems give up so easily on the students needing the most help rather than using the systems inability to educate and graduate Black boys as justification for the adoption and funding of instructional models geared toward educating kinesthetic and tactile learners like vocational schools and arts programs. These models demonstrate the innate abilities of Black boys. How interesting that these program models have been defunded, when they could be instrumental in improving graduation rates and reducing incarceration rates.

In lieu of this national crisis and America's indifference to the state of Black boys, I cannot in good conscience sit idly by praying and marching, while the big bad wolf huffs and puffs and blows away the futures of boys who look like me. The time has come for Black men and women to exit their church buildings and confront the wolf. For institutional racism to exist in a society where over two hundred million men and women profess Christianity speaks to the ineffectiveness of the Christian church.

As the founder of the New Testament Church, Jesus commanded his disciples to "*GO*" and make disciples of all nations. This is the Mission of the Church: to "*GO*" and make disciples. By making disciples of all nations, Jesus expected his followers to create a kingdom on earth that would operate like the spiritual kingdom in heaven. This kingdom would function independently of race and ethnicity. That is why Jesus describes the heavenly kingdom as an inward reality (Luke 17:21). This truth about the heavenly kingdom should inform the church's faith and practice. If we expect to create a world where people are not judged by color of their skin, but by the content of their character, the command to "*GO*" and make disciples must become a living reality, not simply dry ink on paper. The Church has to stop building buildings and start building people. God is not concerned with buildings. He wants to live in people.

This is the only real solution for ending racism and reducing the racial disparities and mortality rates resulting from it. We must somehow convert the hearts of men with spiritual truth and unconditional love. By spiritual truth, I am not suggesting that we convert racist people to the Christian faith, because most people advocating white supremacy already profess Christianity. True spirituality is not a religion, but rather an awareness of the fact that who and what we are transcends any race or ethnicity we espouse to. We are first and foremost spiritual beings. This is paramount. Through unconditional love or the commitment to deny self-interest to do what is in the best interest of others, we can collectively eradicate race prejudice. After all, what other alternatives do we have? Politicians will never solve the issue of racism. In truth, no amount of legislation—despite its intent—will ever change a racist heart.

Therefore, I am inclined to use this literary platform to evoke real dialogue between the races to dispel the myth that Black boys are inherently bad deserving of self-contained classrooms, psychiatric drugs, out of school suspensions, and locked facilities. Having this conversation is not only important, but also necessary for creating real and sustainable change. Once we embrace the true essence of our spiritual nature we can eradicate race prejudice and create a springboard from which to launch a shared vision of truly leaving no child behind, for indeed we are one.

The New Plantation

From nigger to minority, labeled by the majority, sweet land of liberty to thee I cannot sing.

Slave ships, leather whips, educationally ill equipped to reap your monetary profits. I renounce the legitimacy of my citizenship until freedom truly rings.

Drug dealers dressed in lab coats, creating synthetic antidotes, a billion-dollar scapegoat are children born in black coats. Our chance for freedom is remote, independent of the black vote.

And we ask ourselves why the African fails in desegregated schools. Because his presence is a historical absence, he has no significant frame of reference, other than the texts that present him as unintelligent.

How can he be expected to succeed, when all he reads reflecting good deeds, depicts the empowerment of another peoples' seed? Herein lies the need for the African's mind to be freed.

Part 1:
The Matter At Hand

Killing the Dream

"Imagine this: You are taken into a room and made to sit on a hard, wooden chair with a desk in front of it. You are not allowed to eat, drink, speak, or go to the bathroom. You are expected to stay in this room for six hours. There will be two breaks, 10 and 30 minutes. if you cannot follow these rules, you are given psychiatric drugs to control your behavior. Where are you? In a prison? No, you are in an American public elementary school."[1]

- Dr. Jawanza Kunjufu

Somewhere between preschool and 5th grade something traumatic happens to little Black boys; something that I believe should never happen to any child. Their love for learning diminishes. Their spirit is broken. That same little boy who once dreamed of being someone great—positively impacting his community like his favorite superhero—has for some reason lost interest in school believing that he is stupid, dumb, and incapable of learning. He begins seeing himself as a behavior problem that his teacher must confine and contain so that he does not disrupt the learning process for the "smart children." This is the reality for many Black boys.

The good news, however, is that we can change this reality, but we must be willing to ask the hard questions like: "What killed these boys dreams? What happened to make them lose faith in their invisibility?" What happened to them wanting to become Black astronauts, doctors, scientists, and lawyers? Why is the burial ground of murdered aspirations filled with the hopes and dreams of little Black boys? Is it the result of culturally incompetent frustrated teachers referring them to child study teams for testing, or could it be the deficit based labels and self-contained classrooms?

Is it the excessive suspensions written by punitive minded administrators for minor infractions? Or do we contribute it to neglectful parents who sit idly by indulging their children with excessive television watching and playing video games as opposed to making them study and complete homework assignments? I am not professing to have all the answers, but I do believe that public school systems are assassinating dreams along with the dreamers and it is becoming a national epidemic.

Whereas at one time these boys were eager to learn, filled with energy and excitement, their experiences inside public school buildings have for some reason created a deep seated hatred for learning as evidenced by the number of Black boys dropping out of America's classrooms. This mass exodus of Black boys departing from the public school system is a travesty. If White boys were dropping out at these same rates, America would band together and flood the nation's capital demanding education reform. Mass media circuits would report it every day on radio and television stations. Politicians would pass new laws to address the problem of low-test scores, excessive dropout rates, and correctional placements.

So why hasn't the country demanded the same for Black boys? Why is there not a national outcry to address these racial disparities? The call to rise up and advocate for Black boys is upon us! No longer can we expect institutions bent on perpetuating their mental enslavement and collective disenfranchisement to be the answer for them obtaining a brighter future. We must be proactive in creating an intentional future for our boys. If there was ever a time in history that a people needed to act, this is it. Our boys are depending on us.

I challenge every leader in the Black community to research the word "Leader" in the dictionary. It means, "To go first!" If we expect excellence from our boys, adults must model the expectation. We must ask ourselves, have we given them excellence or have we stood on the sidelines criticizing and condemning them? This should be the litmus test for society as a whole. How can we as a nation demand "A's" from these boys when we are content with them living an "F" lifestyle? Even Jesus said those that are well have no need of a physician. He focused his attention on the less fortunate. Black boys are the "sick ones" of modern society. Their spirit is broken and their minds are shackled. These are the ones in need of assistance.

Oh how I long for the day when the crooked places shall be made straight, the rough places plain, and the valleys exalted! Understand that our failure to act in our boys' best interest will ultimately result in them becoming a permanent underclass. Now is the time for us to invoke the spirit and wisdom of our ancestors. I challenge every reader to join me in speaking out against the murderers of our sons' dreams. May the words of Voltaire speak to your heart: *"Every man is guilty of all the good he did not do."*

---

1. Kunjufu, pg. xii

Reflective Questions

1. List some ways you can help your son's dreams alive?

_____
_____
_____
_____
_____
_____

2. What would Jesus do today to address the state of Black boys? Share your answers with your local Church.

_____
_____
_____
_____
_____
_____

3. How can you as a parent serve as a leader to change the state of Black boys in your community?

_____
_____
_____
_____
_____
_____

IDEA: Individuals Destroying Educational Aspirations

"Imagination is more important than knowledge."

- Albert Einstein

  Racing into the school building to meet their new teacher are pre-kindergartners who for the first time, will experience what it is like to be inside a public school classroom. With their shirts hanging off their shoulder and book bags sliding down their arms, the anticipation is too great to slow down the rapid pace of little feet hurrying into the building. Imagine the anxiety of parents who drive off to work entrusting the future and education of their children to teachers they recently met at a back to school night. The feeling, I'm sure, can be a little unsettling. What that child is to become in life will be greatly impacted by the quality of instruction he receives from the teacher with whom he spends seven to eight hours of his day, Monday through Friday. But what happens once that child enters the classroom for the first time?

  The classroom bursts with bright colors, letters, shapes, pictures, and toys that excite his mind and encourage his curiosity and exploration as neurons fire rapidly and little hands move excitedly and uncontrollably. Learning at this stage is fun and amazing and children, independent of their neighborhood and socioeconomic status, love it. The sky is their limit. Their expectations are high and the world is their playground. They have no preconceived understanding about student learning disabilities or classroom etiquette. It is the first day of school and learning for them is adventurous! They are eager, present and accounted for, and ready to learn.

As inquisitive sponges, these boys are raring to soak up every bit of knowledge their environment affords them. Sitting down and being quiet, while part of classroom decorum is not an option for these touchy feely learners whose minds are over stimulated by the wealth of information surrounding them. They have no prejudices about their teacher or her unwillingness to treat all children equitably. Nor can they comprehend a burned out teacher whose motivation for being there is three more years until retirement so she bothers easily of the slightest movement of an energetic child. They are not sophisticated enough in their thinking process to understand why a college educated teacher would spend more time writing office referrals than differentiating her instruction to accommodate their unique learning style. It is not until she has bounced them back and forth between other teachers that they begin developing a dislike and distrust for the one place responsible for their cognitive development.

Parents, does any of this sound familiar to you? Have you experienced this scenario with your son's school? I bet right now there are teachers that come to mind as you read this chapter. Am I right? Don't worry you are not alone. I have been there and some of you are still there. You often wonder why are these teachers still employed? If they are not fond of working with black students, why don't they transfer to another school? Do you have this silent conversation too? You see and hear teachers yelling at Black boys and sending them out of the classroom for the smallest offense. This is something I witnessed early in my career as a Behavior Modification Technician (BMT) in the public school system.

As a BMT, it was my job to control the unruly Black students in self-contained classrooms so the mainstreamed white students could learn without disruption. The schools at which I worked were made up of large free and reduced lunch or economically disadvantaged student populations and operated like slave plantations. White administrators would hire Black taskmasters to control the rebellious field hands. Those Black students who demonstrated a modest level of academic potential enjoyed the comforts of a mainstream classroom as long as they understood that their being there was a privilege and acted accordingly. In this particular setting, I acted as a Black Uncle Tom controlling the behavior of my people to appease White slave master administrators.

Michael Porter author of *Kill Them Before They Grow*, depicts this Uncle Tom behavior as paycheck slavery: Blacks remaining quiet about institutional neglect and mistreatment of Black students to maintain a paycheck.[1] That description fit me to a T. Like most Blacks within the public school system, I kept quiet and actively participated in removing Black boys from mainstream classrooms to maintain a steady income. There were several times when I witnessed teachers send disrespectful White students to the guidance counselor's office to cool down, while referring Black boys who committed a similar offense to the principal's office because the behavior of the latter was considered disruptive or disrespectful. This is how teachers justified having Black boys removed from their classrooms and placed in self-contained environments. They understood that if they removed the child from their classroom enough times they had justification for initiating the process of having him placed in a separate learning environment. I witnessed these accounts firsthand in numerous schools.

Then at intervention meetings these same teachers would sit around the table smiling at uneducated parents like Cheshire cats trying to convince them that the process of moving their son into a self-contained classroom with a smaller teacher to student ratio and an assistant was in their son's best interest. They would often sell the parents on the idea that their son would receive more services. And since teachers use educational jargon and acronyms unfamiliar to "non-school" folk, parents would sign whatever forms school staff placed in front of them believing they were doing what was best for their son. I guess seeing Black faces around the table sent a message to parents that what the school was proposing could not be that bad if people of color were taking part in the process. I feel dirty even thinking about it.

As a parent, it is necessary for you to understand that schools are mandated to identify, locate, and evaluate all children with disabilities. This process is called "Child Find." Yes, Local Educational Agencies actually have a process in place to identify children with disabilities. This process on the outside looks good because it provides a system for identifying and assisting students with medically valid disabilities who require additional supports to take advantage of a free and appropriate public education. However, a look further into the spirit of the letter will reveal that this policy also creates a covert way for a racist system to target Black boys and refer them to a process that will result in their misdiagnosis and mis-education. Let's examine how this process works.

First, the student must be identified as possibly having a learning disability. Next, school personnel may use a process called Response To Intervention (RTI) as a pre-referral process to determine if it is necessary to refer the student for a formal evaluation for special education services. If it is determined that a formal evaluation for special education services is warranted, consent from the parent or guardian must be received.[2] Upon receipt of the parents' signature, IDEA sets a timeframe of 60 days for schools to complete the evaluation although the timeframe can vary from state to state. A school psychologist completes and reviews the results of the evaluation (e.g., academic, behavioral/emotional, and cognitive functioning) and determines whether or not the child is eligible for services. If the child is determined to be eligible for special education services as defined by IDEA legislation, an Individualized Education Program (IEP) meeting is scheduled and conducted. Out of this meeting, the IEP is created and the child begins receiving special education services based on this plan.[3]

If parents only knew that by signing those forms they were consenting to a process that would result in their son being evaluated for a nonmedical diagnosis, labeled with a deficit-based pathology, placed on psychiatric drugs, and placed in a setting that would make it extremely difficult for their son to be successful in school. Armed with these facts, I don't think any parent would actively participate in this process of educational demise. That is exactly what special education amounts to for boys of color. It is a system that ultimately leads to their destruction.

Dr. Jawanza Kunjufu, a national educational consultant, provides evidence of this in his article on Black boys in special education. He points out that only 27 percent of the 6.4 million students in the 60 billion dollar special education industry graduate from high school.[4] Think about what this means for the majority of Black boys in self-contained classrooms. By agreeing to have their son tested, parents are acting as accomplices in the murder of their son's dreams. That is why parents should make sure the school has exhausted every resource possible before testing their child. The outcomes more often than not are stacked against him. Likewise, parents can assess their child's behavior in other settings (home, church, social outings etc.) to make sure that the patterns of behavior that the school has documented are consistent across settings. If your son truly has a learning disability, the same behavior patterns should manifest across home, school, and community. Take accurate notes and share your observations with the school. No diagnosis should be made based solely on what the school observes. Observations should be "objective" not "subjective." You cannot entrust your son's future to a system that has proven ineffective for boys of color.

Unfortunately, many parents are unaware of how the proponents of white supremacy have taken on a totally different approach to racism by removing "Whites only" signs from public places and incorporating their separatist ideology into public policy. This is the new Jim Crow. Understand that the White power structure of the Jim Crow era has transferred the Laws of 1876-1965 from public places to public policy as evidenced by the widening gap in public education between "Whites only" gifted and talented placements and "Black" self-contained, special education placements. Black boys are the poster children for America's uneducable student population. We must reverse this negative trend.

Consider the fact that there are 97,000 public schools in America with an enrollment of 49 million students. Of the students enrolled, Blacks represent 16% of the student population, while Whites represent 51% of public school students.[5] And although Blacks represent a minority in public school enrollment, they are "overrepresented" in special education placements. According to Dr. Kunjufu, Black students make up 30 percent of America's special education placements and 80 percent of those placements are Black males! This is separatism disguised as "educational policy." How can the public school system label this overrepresentation of Black boys in special education anything other than institutional neglect and abuse, especially when we witness the same disproportionality in school discipline records?

Black boys only account for 9 percent of America's public school students, yet they make up 24 percent of students suspended and 30 percent of public school students' expelled.[6] Similar are the findings for disproportionality in the criminal justice system. Black youth make up 44% of youth who are detained, 46% of the youth who are judicially waived to criminal court, and 58% of the youth admitted to state prisons.[7] Do you think this coincidental or intentional? And what are the consequences of juvenile justice agencies placing these nonviolent offenders in locked facilities? Their involvement in the criminal justice system minimizes the likelihood of them going to college and becoming gainfully employed, which leads to their deeper involvement in the judicial system. Thus it becomes a cycle of miseducation (curriculums of genocide, suspensions, and arrests), incarceration, and unemployment, which perpetuates a vicious cycle of youth going in and out of locked facilities (recidivism).

How unfortunate that America would allocate more dollars to incarcerating their youth than investing taxpayer dollars in improving the quality of education and expanding school resources to address the non-academic barriers that negatively impact student learning. Jailing young people is not cost-effective. It costs state and local governments as much as $21 billion annually for these punitive placements. Locking up a juvenile cost states an average of $407.58 per person per day and $148,767 per person per year.[8] States don't spend anywhere near this amount on education. Nationwide, states spent an average of $10,667 per student in the 2011-12 school year – a 2.8 percent drop from the $10,975 they spent in 2010-11.[9] You do the math.

Based on the numbers, America could educate fourteen students for the cost of incarcerating one. The national slogan should be "It is cheaper to educate than incarcerate!" So why do you think America spends more money on punitive strategies that are counterproductive when they could spend less and produce better results? Could it be because the majority of its incarcerated youth are boys of color? Again I ask, "Is it a systematic plot to destroy Black boys?" I'll let you be the judge; but before you label me a conspiracy theorist, understand that the negative overrepresentation of Black boys continues into adulthood.

A recent article indicated that Black males in America, ages 18 and older, account for 5.5% of all college students, but 1 million of the 2.3 million incarcerated. The same article went on to say that 49% of African American males had been arrested before their 23rd birthday.[10] This is the state of Black males in America. These racial disparities are further exacerbated by the fact that there are more Black men in the prison system today than there were slaves in 1850 under chattel slavery.[11] Evidently, America has found a way to reintroduce slavery through cheap prison labor. Did you know that the United States is only 5% of the world's population, but has 25% of the world's prison population? Prisons in America are private business enterprises and our government guarantees these private corporations a 90% occupancy rate![12] Thus we have justification for the school to prison pipeline.

This systemic issue of targeting Black boys for future prison beds is motivated by racism and greed. It is the direct result of White supremacists creating new ways to contain and confine Black males, while reinventing the economic surplus of chattel slavery. By utilizing corporate lobbyists to argue for zero tolerance school policies, mandatory sentencing laws, and three strike rules; White America continues to capture Black males and profit off their labor. Sad to say, but institutional slavery is big business in America and on Wall Street! Shame on you America! Certainly, this is an issue that every Person of Color and Person of Concern must address collectively if we hope to reverse these negative trends.

What we are witnessing today is nothing short of the Jim Crow era reinvented. The only difference between now and then is that the White power structure of today practices racism through public policy. The system today is more covert. It is the Old South masquerading in a new dress. In similar fashion to the racist South and its separate but equal treatment for Blacks, school districts across the country are maintaining a philosophy of separatism. It is special education and incarceration for Blacks and gifted and talented placements for Whites. Just like how the racist South relegated Blacks to second-class citizens and forbade them to use the same public places as Whites, the public school system is placing Black boys in self-contained classrooms and restricting their access to a mainstream education because the system has labeled them dangerous and uneducable. The fact that the public school system designed a way to segregate children cannot be denied when you read the Education For All Handicapped Children Act (Public Law 94-142) that President Gerald Ford signed into law in 1975.[13]

According to Public Law 94-142, all children are guaranteed the right to receive a free public education. This meant that previously omitted students' would be granted access into America's classrooms independent of their disability. Based on this piece of legislation it would appear that America was making strides in creating an equitable playing field for all children independent of their disability. But as history demonstrates, legislation alone can't change a racist system. While Public Law 94-142 opened doors for children with disabilities, it created a means for public school systems to remove Black boys from mainstream classrooms. From this law, America introduced special education as an alternative to mainstream instruction.

So while Public Law 94-142 permitted students with disabilities access into public school classrooms, it also introduced a way for America to once again racially segregate its students into separate, restrictive learning environments.

Congress later revised and classified this law in 1990, under the new name Individuals with Disabilities Educational Act (IDEA).[14] It was an IDEA created by White supremacists to strengthen the IDEA of keeping public school students racially segregated. By labeling students with nonmedical diagnoses like Attention Deficit Disorder, Attention Deficit Hyperactivity Disorder, and Emotional Behavioral Disturbance, schools were able to deny Black boys access into mainstream classrooms. This was a deliberate attempt to circumvent Section 601 of the Civil Rights Act of 1964 that specifically states, *"No person in the United States shall, on the ground of race, color, or national origin, be excluded from participation in, be denied the benefits of, or be subjected to discrimination under any program or activity receiving Federal financial assistance."*[15] Despite this legislation, the public school system, through the creation of nonmedical diagnoses and deficit-based labels, continued to disregard the Civil Rights Act as evidenced by the overrepresentation of Black boys in special education. As I stated earlier, Black boys make up only nine percent of the public school population, but they more than double that percentage in mentally uneducable placements. This is educational genocide and proves what I have been saying all along, that legislation alone cannot change a racist system. Only a renewal of the heart and mind can eradicate racism.

We further witness the inequities of the public school system in their deliberate attempt to prevent Black boys from graduating with a high school diploma. Did you know that many states have adopted policies that make it extremely difficult for students with disabilities to gain access to a four-year college? By creating diploma options for students with disabilities other than a traditional high school diploma, public school systems ensure that your son will not be college ready. Beware of these alternative diplomas. Here are few that I have researched:

IDEA: Individuals Destroying Educational Aspirations

1.) Technical Diploma: Awarded in 11 states to those who complete greater numbers of units in certain subject areas, complete a series of courses in a technical field, attain certain scores on technical assessments, or obtain technical certification before completing high school.

2.) IEP/Special Education Diploma: Awarded in 10 states for special education students in which graduation requirements are set forth in the IEP.

3.) Certificates of Attendance or Achievement: Awarded in 26 states to students who do not have the grades or other requirements (such as passing high school exit exams) needed for a diploma, but who have completed a set number of classes or met sufficient attendance.[16]

Most parents are unaware of the various graduation tracks and simply entrust these matters to the guidance staff at their son's school. This is a gross error on parents' part. As a parent you have to familiarize yourself with the graduation requirements for your son's high school and advocate for him being placed back into a mainstream setting if he is currently in a self-contained classroom. The goal is to make sure your son meets the necessary criteria for graduating with a traditional high school diploma. Once he returns to the mainstream classroom, make sure his courses are both academically rigorous and lead to him completing the necessary course of study for admission to a four-year college. This is important because college admission officers assess your son's transcript based on the academic rigor of his courses and successful completion of his high school credit hours. Your son could be bringing home straight A's in his classes, but if those classes are not standard high school courses that colleges look for, there is a strong possibility that he will not be eligible to attend a four-year institution. I suggest that parents contact the nearest four-year college or university and schedule a campus tour. While there, ask the admissions staff what high school courses are required for students seeking admission to their school. This may differ with universities but at least you will have a general ideal of what your son should be taking.

Once you have the necessary course requirements, schedule an appointment with your son's guidance counselor and advocate for him to be placed in the appropriate high school classes so he can obtain those credits. And if you have a younger son, make sure his teacher is providing him with the necessary foundations to take those classes in high school. The appropriate time to have this discussion is at a parent-teacher conference. These conferences are designed for parents to actively inquire about their child's academic progress. At the meeting, you want to ask the teacher if your son is functioning on grade level in the core content areas of reading and math. If he is below grade level, ask the teacher how she differentiates her instruction to meet the needs of her struggling students. Ask her about the resources the school offers to its low performing students. Inquire about websites and strategies that parents can use at home to address academic deficiencies. Get involved in your son's education!

Your goal as a parent is to make sure your son is performing at or above grade level. As Malcolm X said, "By any means necessary!" You cannot wait until your son's senior year of high school to get involved. Getting involved at the high school level is like waiting for the water company to turn off your water before paying the bill. Preparing your son for academic success starts at the elementary level making sure he has a firm grasp on phonetic awareness, reading comprehension, and reading fluency, along with the basic mathematical modes of operation: addition, subtraction, multiplication, and division. Learning is sequential: he cannot move to "B" until he has mastered "A."

The first step is creating a home environment conducive for learning. This is crucial to your son's educational advancement. Music Videos, Play Station, and social media cannot consume the majority of his time if you expect him to perform well in school and graduate. The educating of our boys must become a priority if we expect to see more of them attending four-year colleges and occupying leadership positions at the national level. That means exposing them to higher learning early. It means parents taking their sons' to as many college activities as possible so that being on a college campus feels natural. We must get to a place, as a people, where higher education is a basic expectation for all of our boys. Seeking knowledge has to be one of our core values so that our boys will develop a high level of respect for the classroom. By respect, I mean they hold it in high regard as the primary place responsible for mobilizing them from poverty to affluence. This will help reduce the numbers of Black boys placed in special education and youth correctional facilities. It will also help reinstate their dreams of being more than an athlete or a rapper. This is my hope for this generation.

Even as I sit here tonight typing these sentences, I am convinced now, more than ever, that we must hold education in high regard, considering the fact that only 11 percent of Black students met three or more standards on the 2014 ACT college readiness test compared to 49 percent of White students.[17] Similar were their outcomes on the 2013 SAT. Only fifteen percent of Black students met or exceeded the SAT benchmark for college and career readiness.[18] We must do better as a people and employ the resources in our local communities to close this achievement gap. This means partnering with local nonprofits and colleges to hold SAT and ACT prep courses at our local churches and partnering with the local banks to come in and teach financial literacy so we can eradicate intergenerational poverty. It also means bringing in agencies that can discuss first time home ownership programs for parents living in low-income housing. This approach to wrapping services around youth and families will aid in creating self-sufficiency and empowerment for our disenfranchised communities. This is a vital step for developing our boys into strong Black leaders.

The church must also become actively involved in this process by making attendance in these programs and services mandatory for every parent and Black boy in their congregation. I assign this task to the church because the church is the one place where members of the Black community gather collectively and consistently to receive information that improves their way of life. The importance of education in our homes and churches is something Pastors must articulate consistently as well as holding parents and the school system accountable for the academic outcomes of all children. It also means that parents and the church display a consistent presence at parent-teacher conferences and become actively involved in helping our boys' function at or above grade level in the core content areas of reading and math. These are but a few steps to ensuring our sons graduate from high school with the necessary skills to be admitted to a four-year college or university.

―――――――――――――――――――

1. Porter, pg. 13

2. Right to an Evaluation of a Child for Special Education Services, Web.

3. 10 Basic Steps in Special Education, Web.

4. Kunjufu, Web.

5. Lee, Web.

6. BrainstormUSA Blog, Web.

7. Criminal Justice Fact Sheet, Web.

8. Sneed, Web.

9. Bidwell, Web.

10. Feierman, Web.

11. Mulvaney, Web.

12. Hodges, Web.

13. Moody, Web.

14. Fitzgerald, Web.

15. Title IV Statute, Web.

16. Fact Sheet: High School Diploma Options Offered In Other States, Web.

17. Tyson, Web

18. Sanchez, Web.

Reflective Questions

1. What can you do at home to ensure your son is proficient in reading and math?

_____
_____
_____
_____
_____
_____

2. What high school courses does your son need to take to be eligible for enrollment in a four-year college or university?

_____
_____
_____
_____
_____
_____

3. What SAT and ACT events do the colleges in your community offer high school students?

_____
_____
_____
_____
_____
_____

Black Boys: Public Enemy Number One

Parents, before you proceed with this chapter, I want to share something with you that a high school administrator shared with me a couple years ago during one of our closed-door conversations. His exact words were, *"The failure of Black boys in public schools is not coincidental. It is intentional and by design. We cannot label something of this magnitude and affecting an entire race of people as a chance occurrence."* Needless to say, I agreed with his assessment.

In 1859, Charles Darwin introduced his Theory of Evolution based on the Natural Selection. According to Darwin, genetics play a major role in determining the survivability and extinction of a particular species.[1] This is vital for Black parents to understand when considering the motive behind the mental destruction and murder of Black boys. Self-preservation is the first law of nature. We will do whatever it takes to preserve our life. It is an innate response, a survival mechanism. Fear of extinction produces radical measures. So White America preserving their own kind is not only natural, but indicative of what drives the racism we witness in most governmental institutions. Therefore, targeting Black boys for destruction is about more than skin color. It's about the majority race in America fearing a loss of power and possible extinction. This fear results in whites creating policies that keep Black boys ignorant and ineligible to compete for a seat at the decision-making table. This is racism at its core: a philosophy predicated on fear.

As a matter of fact, during a recent interview with Tavis Smiley, Fox News host, Bill O'Reilly actually stated that Blacks scare the White power structure.[2] Talk about a Freudian slip! This is the unrealized power that

Black boys have. They pose a very real threat to White America. If allowed to develop into productive citizens, Black boys will become weapons of mass destruction. And I don't mean this in a violent sense. Black males are the carriers of the dominant genes. The recessive genes majority understands this and as such must destroy them during their developmental years by implementing strategies that will bring about their collective demise. This is why public policy will never favor the advancement of the Black male. Every policy is created to destroy him. School systems must **MIS-EDUCATE** him. If he cannot read or grasp the basic modes of mathematics, he will have difficulty graduating from high school and obtaining gainful employment resulting in him engaging in criminal activity to meet his basic needs. This will eventually lead to his arrest and involvement with the penal system.

Upon receiving him into their custody, judicial agencies must **INCARCERATE** him. It should be apparent at this point that the disproportionate numbers of Black males in the penal system is not a coincidence. It is projected that 1 out of every 3 Black males will go to prison in his lifetime.[3] This is not a conspiracy theory, these strategies have been thought out and proven to be very effective. If your son is not reading proficient in the elementary years, his chance for academic success declines greatly. That factor alone makes him a prime candidate for the penal system considering the fact that 85 percent of all juvenile offenders are illiterate and more than 70 percent of the prison population cannot read above a fourth grade level.[4] So what does this mean for you? Once these social institutions portray your son as unintelligent and delinquent, law enforcement now is justified in committing his homicide resulting in your son being **ANNIHILATED**.

If nothing else motivates you as a parent to sit down with your son and help him master phonetic awareness and reading fluency and comprehension, the increased likelihood of him ending up in America's school to prison pipeline should be the kick in the pants you need to become an active participant in your son's education. And here is another sobering thought for parents whose sons' end up in adult facilities. After the penal system labels your son a convicted felon, his chance of living a normal life is negatively impacted. Contrary to popular belief, felons never pay their debt to society despite what the justice system would have you believe.

The sad reality is that a convicted felon has a better chance of hitting the lottery than landing a decent job. By decent, I mean a wage that will allow him to provide for a family. Given that fact, answer me this parents, "If your son pays his debt to society by serving his time and upon release he cannot obtain gainful employment because of his conviction, how long will it be before he returns to a life of crime to make ends meet?" Get the point? For America to incarcerate nonviolent offenders is a deliberate conspiracy of the White power structure to eliminate its Black competition and maximize the corporate wealth of its private prisons through cheap labor or the institutional slave trade. It is an agenda driven by fear and greed. That is why Black boys are more likely to be convicted than their white counterparts even if both groups commit similar offenses. Incarceration is a means of containing that segment of the population that poses a real threat to White America's survival, while at the same time maintaining a profitable enterprise like the good old days.

The powers that be understand that poverty and a lack of basic education is the best way to control and contain a people. Keep them poor and uneducated and you reduce their chance of posing a viable threat. Without a high school diploma, the chances of your son having some level of involvement with the penal system greatly increases, resulting in his confinement. It starts with the public school system relying on suspensions and resource officers for minor infractions that result in him missing an excessive number of instructional days and failing to meet proficiency standards for graduation. This forces him out of the schoolhouse into the jailhouse. From there it is a revolving door or what the judicial system calls recidivism.

Policymakers have thought this through and planned for your son's future, which is why some believe that states use fourth grade reading scores to project the number of future prison beds. And while some may dismiss this as a conspiracy theory, parents would do well to compare what is happening to Black boys in America to the story of the Hebrew males in Exodus. The strategy is exactly the same. If you target the male for destruction, it limits procreation and racial advancement.

In the book of Exodus, we read about how the Egyptian government used racial genocide to destroy the sons of a slave race that resided in their land. According to the story, Pharaoh became worried about the growing number of Hebrews and their ability to unify and overtake the present power structure. This fear resulted in him decreeing policies that targeted all the Hebrew males. He implemented social policies at the local level that would adversely affect those living in the poor neighborhoods. Understand that these policies were designed to prevent Hebrew boys from growing up into strong Black men who could challenge Egyptian sovereignty. In other words, fear drove Pharaoh to take extreme measures to stop the advancement of another racial group.

Think about how closely the Exodus story mirrors what is happening to Black boys in America. The American government, by creating racist policies, has targeted Black males for mass destruction. They want to eliminate your son's chances of challenging their social, political, and economic standing. And electing a Black President only worsened the matter. Whereas at one time the goal was to mis-educate and incarcerate, electing a Black President has now accelerated their agenda and Black males must be annihilated. If the mental destruction fails in keeping your son in his place, he must be annihilated. This is the national decree and governmental workers in blue uniforms are carrying out their orders. But they are not alone in carrying out the execution of Black boys.

Every child service agency in America is charged with carrying out federal mandates that keep the poor dependent on governmental assistance. Their goal is never to promote self-sufficiency. For Black boys to function independent of formal service providers would result in them having too much power and control. Therefore, government agencies, comprised mostly of White women, must enforce policies that destroy Black boys from birth. From poor healthcare and nutrition to mis-education and incarceration, the government has mandated their workers to mis-educate, incarcerate, and annihilate your son. They must make sure he is not equipped with the knowledge to challenge the existing power structure. That is why it behooves you as a parent to make sure your son receives proper prenatal care, nutritional services, social skills activities, and preschool services. You cannot afford to neglect this responsibility. Proverbs 22:6 states that parents are to train up their children. The conspiracy to destroy your son is real and governmental agencies are targeting him from birth. You must be his biggest advocate. Exodus teaches us that powerful things can happen when a mother advocates for her son.

Jochebed, the mother of young Moses, was well aware of the government's conspiracy to destroy her son, but rather than passively accept her son becoming a victim of ill will, she purposed in her heart that the Egyptian power structure would not kill her son. Being proactive, this mother who was on governmental assistance equipped her son to take advantage of the very system that sought his demise. This mother went to the extent to link her son to a Person of Concern within the Egyptian government who possessed the resources to improve his life. Her action is a revelation for parents. Not everyone in Egypt agreed with Pharaoh's decree. There were individuals who disobeyed the order to assassinate the Hebrew males, which has held true throughout history.

From chattel slavery to the Jim Crow era, there have been what I like to call, People of Concern, that sought to abolish chattel slavery and end racial segregation. That is why at the end of this book I mention the need for People of Color and People of Concern to create a shared vision.

This process requires the collective intelligence and resources of all races and nationalities. As a parent you must be willing to advocate for your son by employing the collective intelligence of all people. Reach out to the local college or university, specifically the Education Chair, and ask them if it is a requirement for undergraduate students to fulfill a certain number of internship hours. If so, inquire about the possibility of using some of those students as after-school tutors at your son's school to assist struggling students in math and reading. Should this be something the chairperson is receptive to doing, schedule a meeting with your son's school to discuss starting an after-school tutoring program in partnership with the college. It would not cost the school any additional money and now they have a community-based partner assisting them in closing the achievement gap and improving their end of year test data. Desperate times call for desperate measures.

We must be willing to advocate and embrace People of Concern to help us in reversing this negative trend of academic failure for Black boys. There are in fact White people in America who agree that the disproportionate number of Black boys placed in special education, their excessive suspension rates, and confinement in penal institutions is alarming. These People of Concern have historically committed to helping right America's wrongs. That is why we must embrace these individuals as part of the solution. We cannot continue playing the role of the victim and allow socioeconomic status and institutional racism to discourage us from acting and soliciting support.

Parents must become resourceful and resilient like Jochebed. This mother was proactive in advocating for her son and went as far as to assign "*In Loco Parentis*"—a Latin phrase for "In the place of a parent," to Pharaoh's daughter. She made sure her son did not become a victim of the system.[5] Because of her advocacy and stubborn optimism; Moses attended school in the king's court. The weapon formed against him did not prosper. He received a scholarship to the Ivy League of his day simply because of his mother's resilience. Think about that for a moment. A low-income mother receiving governmental assistance refused to let her son become a victim of the system. This Hebrew slave understood that the government was conspiring to kill her son. She further understood that their plan was systemic and implemented through racist policies. This mother was savvy in how she welcomed government workers into her home having had knowledge that they were charged to assassinate her son! She is to be admired for her courage and advocacy.

Unfortunate, however, is the fact that these same challenges confront mothers today in the 21st century. America has waged war on your son. He is a national threat that must be eliminated by any means necessary: curriculums of genocide, psychiatric drugs, incarceration, or murder. He is the possessor of genetic material that threaten not only the infrastructure, but the racial identity of White America as evidenced by the anti-miscegenation laws of the late 1600's. According to Merriam Webster's dictionary, "Miscegenation" is a mixture of the races; *especially*: marriage, cohabitation, or sexual intercourse between a White person and a member of another race. This has serious racial implications for the recessive genes majority in this country.

Anti-miscegenation laws or miscegenation laws were used to enforce racial segregation until 1967. These laws criminalized interracial marriage between Blacks and Whites as a way to preclude sexual relationships between White women and Black men.[6] So when we see Black boys negatively overrepresented in special education placements, and correctional facilities, it is the direct result of the White power structure doing everything in their power to keep Black males from becoming eligible for the hand of their White Southern belles. They have an inherent need to keep the races separate to preserve their racial identity. The Negro cannot be allowed to marry their women lest the offspring resulting from their union advance the growing numbers of People of Color. That is why in this post-segregated era, government institutions are going out of their way to restrict the upward mobility of your son.

Recent studies indicate that there are more Black males enslaved in correctional facilities today than there were under chattel slavery in the 1850's.[7] The Black male, because of his dominant genes, has to be contained.

White America has no other choice but to make him out to be something disdainful to White women. This means that news stations must portray him as unintelligent, dangerous, and irresponsible. School systems must depict him as uneducable and behaviorally and emotionally disturbed, and courts must find him to be a threat to community safety. This is the reality your son faces every day.

Many of my Black colleagues may challenge me on this, asserting that Black boys are dangerous, criminal minded, and underperforming academically compared to their White counterparts. I will not disagree with their assessment. However, before we consider the behavior, we must out of necessity examine the root cause responsible for shaping these behaviors. Without considering these factors, we are simply dealing with the effects. Change requires us to examine the cause not just observe and discuss the effects.

It is an easy fix to blame our boys for their behavior rather than address the creators of the environment that helped shaped their behavior. If accountability is what we are seeking from our boys, I am all for it, but let's hold both parties accountable for their level of culpability in the current state of Black males. Let's hold legislators and corporate lobbyists accountable for their role in passing policies that lead to Black boys being overrepresented in special education, youth correctional facilities, and unemployment lines. If this is the soil in which America plants these young black seeds, how can we in good conscience judge the tree for not producing fruit? Place these seeds in good soil (classrooms with culturally competent teachers who espouse to high expectations for all students, economically thriving households, and neighborhoods that afford youth an array of positive enrichment activities) and the tree will produce fruit similar to trees placed in the same mineral rich soil. It is highly unlikely that my Black colleagues would agree to this because it would mean examining and exposing racist policies and the unfair distribution of power and resources.

I actually find it disheartening when Black educators say to me, "Osceola stop making excuses for these boys." For them to downplay my position absolves them of their guilt and the part they play in perpetuating our boys' mental destruction. These are typically the same folks who sit around the master's table too damn afraid to open their mouth and speak out against racial injustice for fear of reprisal. They refuse to address the unfair targeting of Black boys for special education services by White teachers except in private conversations or informal Black gatherings, but never in mixed company. That is the reason I voluntarily chose to leave the public school system. Enough was enough. I realized that my remaining silent meant my consent and I no longer consented to what the public school system was doing to boys of color. If a paycheck meant more to me than creating change for boys who looked like me, I did not deserve the freedoms afforded to me by those upon whose shoulders I stood.

The reality is that there are too many Black students being unfairly targeted for suspension and special education as early as Pre-Kindergarten. This practice goes unchallenged as evidenced by the growing number of Black boys in restrictive learning environments and penal institutions. It is another way of destroying them before they have a chance to compete for a real place in America's power structure. From elementary school they encounter culturally incompetent teachers who restrain their excitement and need for movement and freedom of expression. They must comply with rules that tell them to sit down, be quiet, and listen to boring irrelevant content because at the end of the year they must demonstrate proficiency on a state test. By the time they enter the middle grades they have developed a history of office referrals, suspensions, and have been tested, labeled, and medicated resulting in them being placed in a separate learning environment that places them several grades behind their white peers. What a sad commentary.

The classroom was never intended to educate Black boys. Public schools are designed to chew them up and spit them out and Black educators are helping to throw them to the garbage heap. This is unfair and borders on institutional neglect. So in our boys' defense, I will stop making excuses for them when Black folks start addressing the system that is destroying them. Agreed? How can anyone believe it is fair to hold these boys accountable to the same standard as their White counterparts if we do not afford them the same resources and opportunities? If the public school system expects the same outcomes from all students, they must be willing to advocate for all students to be treated equitably.

This means parents must demand equity from all stakeholders: school boards, city and county officials, church leaders, and every other group with a substantial amount of resources that can improve the lives of economically disadvantaged children. We must not be deluded by the fact that there are some Black boys' who achieve in public schools despite their socioeconomic barriers. This does not discount the negative impact that poverty and racism has on educational outcomes. It only speaks to and affirms the innate power of resilient children and families. But here is what I want you to consider, "Why should one group of children be forced to scrape and struggle, when school systems and communities acknowledge that inequity exists between suburban and inner-city schools?" There is no reason for inequity to exist decade after decade for the same race of students unless it is intentional and by design. And we all know from driving through affluent neighborhoods and poor neighborhoods that there are major discrepancies that still resemble the racist South of the 1800's.

School buildings in predominantly white neighborhoods, the (Master's House), look quite different from schools in low-income neighborhoods. Even the libraries and shopping centers look different. However, no one challenges the aesthetic and cultural advantages of living and attending schools in affluent neighborhoods. Seldom do we address how presentation affects the mental development of children. Presentation is everything. The advantages that White children from middle class neighborhoods have over Black children from low-income neighborhoods speak volumes about their self-confidence, positive outlook, and personal achievement. Students from middle class and affluent homes have parents who make education a high priority, while children from poverty have parents who concern themselves with providing their children with the basic necessities of food, shelter, and clothing. These perspectives are quite different and contributes to how a child views the world.

Students in poverty generally attend old dilapidated schools with check cashing businesses, liquor stores, and abandoned buildings in close proximity (Slave Quarters). This is how the world is presented to them and yet we demand the same of them as we do children whose worldview consist of modern school buildings, manicured lawns, and golf courses within gated communities. Would you call this fair and equitable? It's funny how society places the burden to overcome, prevail, and be resilient on the disadvantaged. We expect from Black boys, what public schools have historically been unwilling to give them: Excellence!

----

1. Than, Web.
2. Atlanta Blackstar, Web.
3. Knafo, Web.
4. Crum, Web.
5. In Loco Parentis, Web.
6. Cumminos, Web.
7. Alexander, Web.

Reflective Questions

1. List all of the free resources (e.g., mentoring agencies, after-school programs, clubs etc.) that exist in your community. How can these agencies help provide safety, structure, and supervision?

_____
_____
_____
_____
_____
_____

2. Meet with your church and local colleges to discuss after-school programs can be put in place for struggling students. List them here.

_____
_____
_____
_____
_____
_____

3. What local businesses can you meet with to discuss partnering with your son's school to expand student resources?

_____
_____
_____
_____
_____
_____

Part 2: What Teachers And Administrators Can Do

Differentiated Instruction Disorder

This chapter is dedicated to the 3.7 million fulltime teachers employed by public school systems around the country.[1] Since you have spent time in the classroom instructing students, I am sure you are familiar with the term "pedagogy." By definition pedagogy is the process of teaching.[2] It describes the instructional strategies used by classroom teachers. In this chapter I want to explore the relationship between pedagogy and Asperger's. The term Asperger's describes a form of autism that displays the characteristics of a restrictive and repetitive pattern of behavior.[3] I intentionally married these two terms because I believe this pairing describes the lack of differentiation that takes place in most public school classrooms.

Unfortunately, the classroom is the one place in America where thinking outside the box is more often than not strongly discouraged. If the system is to be successful in producing a "Black boy model," its teachers must follow instructions. If they go contrary to the instructions, the system will have failed to accomplish its objective. Understand? This fact alone hinders teachers from addressing the needs of students who show up possessing different learning styles. It also demonstrates the ineffectiveness of a one-size fits all instructional model. The fact that the public school system is regimented in its instructional model speaks to the dysfunction of the entire system. If the mission of the public school system is to educate all children and the current methods are failing a certain subgroup of students, wouldn't it make sense to try a different approach? Ignoring this basic fact is a fundamental flaw that has hindered public education from achieving its mission with boys of color. It also raises the question, is the system designed to educate Black boys or is their failure in America's classrooms intentional?

In any manufacturing industry, the goal is to create a quality product. To ensure that quality products are produced, manufacturers task research and development teams with assessing and improving the manufacturing process. This cycle for ensuring quality consist of teams ASSESSING, DIAGNOSING, and PRESCRIBING. This is business 101. So why is it that the educational industry, whose mission is to produce educated children, hasn't employed the collective intelligence of its educators to improve the manufacturing process in the classroom? It is evident that the instructional model is broken. So much time is spent focusing on the defective products when it's the manufacturing system that school systems should be evaluating. If we expect to see real change in the products of the public school system, America is going to have to change the way it does business. The amount of time public schools spend assessing standardized test data, discipline data, and free and reduced lunch percentages, can better be utilized by assessing teacher competency and implementing strategies to improve their regimented instructional methods. Likewise, are the number of hours school staff spend in meetings: staff meetings, grade level meetings, and intervention team meetings. This time can be spent convening interdisciplinary teams (mental health, churches, local businesses, colleges, civic groups, etc.) to gain a better understanding of how to address the multiple intelligences of their diverse student body.

The problem in education, based on my experience, is that public school systems are focusing too much of their attention on the wrong things. Superintendents are holding principals accountable for producing positive measurable outcomes for the students in their buildings, in return, principals hold teachers accountable for end of grade tests data, but neither of these two groups have the autonomy to change how the system works despite the fact that their one-size fits all instructional model has proven ineffective for boys of color. Surely, it is time for the educational community to have some serious discussion about the instructional delivery methods of its teachers. This is a conversation that must take place if, as a country, we expect to produce real and sustainable change for Black male students. Within the context of that conversation, the question, "do Black boys really suffer from short attention spans or are they just bored with the material and how their teachers present the content?" needs to be asked. Then the question, "do the behavioral expectations that public schools hold students accountable to equally apply to teachers?" must also be asked. These are valid questions that deserve honest answers.

When a teacher attends a workshop and doodles on her handout, texts on her cell phone, holds sidebar conversations, or steps out into the lobby for a break, is she tested for a disorder? Her behavior certainly meets the characteristics for Attention Deficit Disorder. Why then is she exempt from the process? If testing is in the best interest of students, why isn't it good for teachers? Shouldn't we expect teachers to model what they expect from their students? I think it is unfair to hold children to a higher standard than we do for adults. Leaders go first! The behaviors we see students exhibiting in the classroom are typical responses. It is quite normal for a child's mind to wander if something fails to hold his interest. If a television program does not hold your interest, don't you turn the channel or if the morning sermon is too long, don't you start nodding off? These behaviors do not represent a behavioral disorder despite the majority vote of the American Psychiatric Association that says it is.[4]

The fact of the matter is that not all children learn the same way. That is why differentiation in the classroom is so important. It forces teachers to become creative in planning their lessons so that all students are inspired to learn and exercise their full potential. I urge teachers to stop labeling how Black boys learn as a disability. The ability to recite rap lyrics verbatim and learn to execute difficult basketball and football plays not only demonstrates a student's capacity to learn; it demonstrates his ability to master difficult content. To label these students anything other than brilliant is a disservice to multiple intelligences. If every student responded well to a left-brain instructional model, there would be no need to challenge how teachers delivered their instruction. But what happens when a large number of right-brained students are forced to attend institutions designed and equipped for left brained learners because of mandatory attendance laws? Will they be successful in a system that forces them to suspend their learning style? Will they feel competent if the system labels how they learn a disability? These are the questions we must address before going to the extremes of labeling children with deficit based labels. Process that for a minute.

Is it not a reasonable request to ask teachers to modify how they deliver instruction to boys of color? If a certain group of students don't respond favorably to lectures, ditto sheets, and multiple-choice tests, wouldn't it be logical to incorporate project-based learning, hands-on group projects, and performing arts in the classroom? Too often, schools restrict these types of activities to "special classes" like dance, physical education, and music rather than using these activities to deliver core content. The Ron Clark Academy in Atlanta, Georgia does a great job of integrating music and dance as a way of delivering core content to students. I encourage you to visit the school website and learn about its philosophy on teaching and to watch the videos of teachers and students in action: www.ronclarkacademy.com.

Considering how the country espouses to leaving no child behind, shouldn't school systems exhaust every resource at their disposal before discarding its underperforming students? Sadly, this is not what we see happening in schools around the country. The public school system has created a separate educational environment to address their "square peg" students whose learning style does not fit their "circle peg" classrooms. And so we have what is formally known as special education: an educational system characteristic of deficit-based labels, self-contained learning environments, and the prescribing of mood altering medications for America's biggest threat: Black boys.

The fact that teachers are locked into one method of teaching clearly demonstrates the inflexibility and unwillingness of the public school system to educate its Black male students. Inflexibility is the last thing a national system serving diverse groups of children should be espousing to. Therefore, the question that needs to be asked is "Who has a learning disability, is it Black boys or the public school system?" I feel comfortable in saying the public school system, which explains its learning disability: Pedagogical Asperger's.

How is it that toy companies, coaches, and movie directors can hold Black boys attention and college educated teachers cannot? This is a simple question. It seems to me that the only place Black boys seem to have attention deficit disorder with or without hyperactivity is in America's regimented classrooms where right brained learners are forced to sit in left-brained classrooms. It is like me trying to slide my size 11-feet into a size 8-shoe. It wouldn't work because it is not a good fit. The same is true for students whose learning style differs from that of the traditional classroom: it is not a good fit. Every child has strengths and capabilities that teachers must identify and develop if all students are to be successful.

Take for example the boys standing on the street corner. Most of them are probably below grade level in reading and math, but still manage to play an intricate role in expanding and sustaining a drug enterprise. They use effective communication skills along with math and science to manufacture, market, and distribute controlled substances to a repeat customer base. Just think about the marketing and mathematical savvy required to handle the number of financial transactions taking place every day on the average street corner. Similar is the level of sophistication these boys exercise in communicating with each other using signs and symbols. It is remarkable how they can retain such comprehensive information in the streets but not in the classroom. So it is obvious that Black boys can learn. In fact, they can thrive if placed in an environment that builds on their strengths. One thing is clear: the streets have developed better teachers and curriculums to equip these boys with the necessary skill sets to be successful in an open market.

Differentiated Instruction Disorder

Street teachers set high expectations for their students and even provide them with opportunities for upward mobility in their drug enterprise. It is amazing how these same boys that schools have removed from mainstream classrooms, because of their inability to stay focused on classroom lessons, can spend hours on task manufacturing, marketing, and selling illegal drugs on the street corner. The question we must ask ourselves is why haven't college educated teachers been able to duplicate the accomplishments of these street teachers? Based on recent graduation statistics, schools are producing the exact opposite, graduating only fifty-nine percent of Black boys from high school.[5] That means a large number of our boys are leaving school ill equipped to participate in the national and global marketplace.

The truth is that public school systems are placing these energetic boys in classrooms where teachers expect them to sit down, be quiet, and complete ditto sheets while listening to dry lectures from passive white female teachers. This environment is not conducive for kinesthetic learners. It is like restricting a racecar to a residential neighborhood. Can we really expect a vehicle with a speedometer of 200+ to perform at its best in a 25mph zone? The ability is there, but without freedom and flexibility it will never maximize its true potential. Sadly, Black boys are often assigned to White female teachers, whose interactions with them are punitive and demeaning thus killing their potential. Notice I used the word "often," because there have been occasions when I have witnessed Black female teachers treating our boys worse than White teachers.

Given this type of framework, how can we expect our boys to be eager about coming to school every day? No sane person would spend time around people who constantly magnified their deficits. People generally gravitate toward environments that validate them. That is why Black boys do so well in school athletics. Despite public school systems diagnosing them with learning disabilities, these boys perform extremely well on the football field and basketball court. Why is that? How can basketball and football coaches inspire our boys to learn and retain complex plays, perform under physically challenging conditions, and demonstrate good sportsmanship on the court for four quarters and licensed teachers have difficulty maintaining them in their classroom for 45 minutes? The difference has to do with how teachers perceive their Black male students and their expectations for them.

When a teacher perceives a child as competent and capable of meeting high expectations, his desire to be validated drives him to meet those expectations. In truth, a teacher's beliefs about race and economics will dictate how she interacts and responds to her students of color. If she believes a boy is unintelligent and a behavior problem, everything he does will be viewed as disruptive and inappropriate. This was the topic of a conference convened in New Jersey back in the late 90's, "Black boys are Bad, White boys are Mad." The underlying philosophy of the conference was the unspoken belief that Black boys who exhibited antisocial behaviors warranted punitive consequences and confinement, while White boys exhibiting the same behaviors warranted counseling and therapy. It was an outgrowth of White folks whose implicit bias about Black boys caused them to prejudge Black boys based solely on their race and ethnicity. They assumed that Black boys were evil and needed to be confined, while their White counterparts were seen as suffering from emotional problems and needed empathy. I wonder how many teachers secretly embrace the belief that Black boys are inherently bad and need to be incarcerated? What a teacher believes about her Black male students will either make or break them—either connecting them to the classroom or driving them to the streets.

If there is one thing I understand, having dropped out of the public school system in the 9th grade to live the street life, it's that children gravitate to environments where learning is achieved by doing. So where are the vocational high schools or the performing arts high schools? And please do not blame it on budget cuts, because there is always enough money to fund new prison beds. Why then is there never enough money to fund new learning centers that prevent delinquency? Prevention is definitely cheaper than intervention. I often hear county and state folk talk about the lack of funding for education year in and year out, but I have yet to hear a judge say there is not enough money to fund the overwhelming number of youth commitments to correctional facilities! Where is the money when it is time to fund vocational education or performing arts programs? Think about that for a minute.

Throughout middle school, my friends considered me a gifted artist. This was in spite of the fact that drawing wasn't a core class. Go figure! Had my teachers taken the time to identify my talents, they would have noticed that Osceola learned differently. I didn't care for ditto sheets and lectures, but put a comic book, pencils, and paper in front of me and I would create a masterpiece worthy of any consumer's dollar. I often wonder what would have happened if my teacher had taken me under her wing and said to me, "Osceola you are going to be a gifted artist someday. I see potential in you so I am going to enter your drawings in an art contest and have the art teacher down the hall mentor you?" What would have happened if that art teacher had exposed me to the various art majors at the college level? How would those interactions have made a difference in whether or not I completed high school? It is amazing what children can do when adults believe in them and link them to the right resources. Unfortunately, that was not the case for me. I had to adapt to a learning style that did not fit.

Consequently, I gave up on school and resorted to hanging on the street corner where I felt valued and appreciated. The moral of the story is, accentuate the positives and stop killing our boys' dreams. Just because they are not good in reading or math does not mean they lack the necessary ability to learn. It simply means that teachers, parents, and community agencies must collectively identify and develop new ways for these boys to learn. Every living organism can learn. This, however, does not seem to be a belief that the public school system practices.

Generally speaking, a lot of teachers kill the creative spirit of their students by confining them to an outdated instructional model. Seldom do they reevaluate their teaching methods to see if they are meeting the needs of the young prodigies sitting before them! It is easier for them to punish the child for refusing to adapt to their instructional model than to differentiate their teaching methods. This punitive philosophy has done nothing but drive a wedge between public schools and Black boys. Ask almost any Black boy who has gotten a few years of public schooling under his belt, what he wants to be when he grows up and more often than not he will respond: a rapper, football player, or basketball player. Why do our boys choose these professions over doctors, scientists, astronauts, and lawyers? It's because athletes and rappers look like them and society celebrates athletes and entertainers. Athletes and rappers get paid a lot of money to play and have fun, something our boys don't associate with the classroom. School is boring to them and if being a doctor, scientist, or lawyer means more schooling, they would rather choose to do something that seems fun, like being a rapper or a professional athlete. To hell with the books!

Energetic children cannot possibly see themselves volunteering for four more years of an experience that has proven to be anything but enjoyable. Another reason Black boys gravitate to music and athletics is because seldom do they see Black lawyers, doctors, or scientists in their neighborhoods. Rapping and athletics are trademarks for boys growing up in poor neighborhoods. This is obvious by the number of parents in attendance at the school during football and basketball season. Teachers may have difficulty getting parents to show up for a parent-teacher conference, but let momma and poppa's baby boy make first string on varsity! Not only will parents show up; if the coach does not give their son ample playing time they will show out! Sports, unlike education, have become the primary vehicle for mobilizing our boys from poverty to middle and upper class.

White-collar occupations do not often establish residency in low-income neighborhoods. Therefore, our boys seldom see doctors, lawyers, or scientists on their block. I guess the goal for a Black man is to make it out of the hood not set up shop there. However, if we want our boys to grow up and aspire to professional occupations, then our Black doctors, lawyers, and scientists are going to have to invest some time in those communities where their presence is lacking. It is only natural that our boys emulate men who look like them and spend time with them. It is not enough just to be a Black man. Just because you are Black does not mean our boys take their cues from you. Boys emulate men they respect and admire.

How many of our boys can relate to men that show up in their business attire driving luxury vehicles to give a fifteen-minute speech for career day? Unless our boys can relate to the men delivering the speeches, their words will fall on deaf ears. That is why I make it a priority to build association with our boys by telling my story. I share with them my upbringing in Miller Homes Housing Projects and my failure to graduate from high school because I took to the street life. Immediately these boys change their perception about me. No longer am I the impressive biography the Principal just read, now I'm the man from around the way dressed up in his Sunday suit! Now I have their attention and an opportunity to share with them how a man that looks like them made it out of the hood by way of a high school education and college degree. See the difference?

Again, our boys pattern themselves after men who look like them and can relate to them. This is true for other species as well. Lions in the jungle grow up emulating other lions in the jungle. It is highly unlikely that a lion in the jungle will pattern himself after a circus lion. They may look the same, but their orientation to life is totally different. With that in mind, it is equally true that Black boys need to be introduced to the African origins of civilization. Failing to educate Black students on the African origins of the arts, sciences, religion, and government is a deliberate attempt of public school systems to make its Black students feel inadequate and historically irrelevant. That is why "knowledge of self" must become a priority for every Black boy.

Parental involvement is key in equipping our boys with an awareness of self and helping them stand against the misinformation of public school curriculums. Without parents exposing their sons to their African ancestors, how will they develop belief in their ability to aspire to greatness? Understand that if the greatest accomplishments we attribute to Black men are the traffic light, peanut butter, and an I Have a Dream speech, how can we expect our boys to compete with boys whose White faces resemble the Savior of the world and the men on US currency? Unfortunately, our boys live in a country where the status symbols of wealth, power, and prestige are linked to a race other than theirs. White America has created this racist system with the hopes of maintaining a slave to slave master relationship. It is intentional and by design. America is using subliminal messages to make Black boys feel inferior without burning a cross or hanging a noose. Remember, pictures are worth a thousand words. That is why church paintings of Jesus, the faces on US currency, and prominent figures in US history books must be of White men.

Disney must make the princes of your child's fairytales White, Christianity has to make the savior of the world White, and America has to make the founders of this nation White! Based on the pictures that school systems and religious groups impose on boys of color, what value do you think they assign to their Black skin in Whitewashed America? Do they see themselves as competitors or do they develop hatred for their black skin? Does this hatred for black skin lead them to murder the possessors of black skin as evidenced by Black on Black homicide being the number one cause of death for Black males between the ages of 15-34?[6] These are some of the questions we must answer if we expect to change the state of Black boys.

Subliminal imagery is killing the spirits of Black boys in America. From the history book to the Disney channel to the church house and schoolhouse, our boys are being programmed to hate themselves. Consequently, this creates an inferiority complex that manifests as low scores on standardized tests, making stupidity and ignorance the rule and being smart the exception. This is the end result of subliminal messages. Movie theaters use this same strategy by displaying dancing refreshments just before the main attraction to evoke thoughts of hunger and thirst. They understand that thought produces behavior. The same is true for the designers of White supremacy. By making the African American male feel historically irrelevant, White supremacists have created the greatest mind control system to ever restrain a race of people.

Therefore, as parents we must do everything in our power to reeducate our sons, to transform their way of thinking, and equip them with the knowledge to combat the negative stereotypes of institutional racism. No longer can we as a people absolve ourselves of the responsibility to teach our own despite the Brown versus the Board of Education decision. We must educate our Black sons! And by educate, I mean more than just disseminate information. We must train them to understand and appreciate their African origins because their thoughts will impact their behavior. As the book of Proverbs teaches, as a man thinks in his heart so he becomes. Who these boys are and what they are to become will be attributed in large part to how they think. This is vital in advancing their spiritual and social standing.

I can vividly recall as a child my father saying to me, son go to school and get a good education so you can get a good job. That is the same advice his father gave to him. His father sent him to a segregated school in the South to get the white folks knowledge. This knowledge, he believed, would mobilize his son from the rural South to middle class suburbia despite the efforts of Jim Crow. Well that may have been true for Black folks back then who had a clear picture of what they were fighting for and the people who were opposing their social advancement, but how do you fight against racism when government institutions embed discriminatory practices within public policy? The fight in this case is not for access to public places but to overturn public policies that unfairly destroy Black boys.

Under Jim Crow, Black people were fighting for the rights that were written in the Constitution. What the Founding Fathers had written guaranteed all men certain inalienable rights. Because of this, Black folks were able to challenge racist practices. In other words, social practices had to align with America's founding documents. So how did the racist south get around the policy issues that threatened to end racism? They simply created policies that justified their social practices. Welcome to the new South where public policy justifies special education and prison industrial complexes for those who have historically been denied their basic inalienable rights under the Constitution!

Similar to the Old South are public school systems that maintain segregated schools by creating separate learning environments for the races: special education for those whom White America wishes to keep disenfranchised and gifted and talented for the offspring of the White power structure. The plan, although unjust and inequitable, is actually quite brilliant. By having media outlets depict Black boys as dangerous and delinquent, public school systems are able to suspend and expel them for minor infractions. Resource officers can arrest them and mental health agencies can conduct subjective assessments to label them with nonmedical diagnoses and prescribe them psychiatric medications. This is a deliberate attempt to destroy Black boys in their developmental years. The White power structure has created a system that not only reserves knowledge and power for "Whites only," it also affords them the ability to maintain the practices of the segregated South.

Public schools are still segregating children as they did in the 1960's as evidenced by the separate learning environments operating inside America's school buildings. As People of Color and People of Concern, we must test our assumptions about the effectiveness of public education for Black boys. I know our parents and grandparents held education and teachers in high regard, but many of them were fortunate enough to receive an education under segregated schooling from Black teachers who were concerned about advancing their race. This is not the case today considering Black teachers only make up 17 percent of the teacher workforce.[7] Worse than that is the fact that Black male teachers make up only 2% of teachers in America.[8] And sad to say, many of the Black teachers are either paycheck slaves or Uncle Toms who treat Black boys harsher than their White counterparts.

The truth of the matter is that many of our Black boys in the public school system are being mistreated and mis-educated by both Black and White teachers. This is very disheartening to say the least. The good news, however, is that despite the failure of many American schools, there are schools producing positive measurable outcomes for boys of color like Urban Prep Academy in Chicago, the Ginn Academy in Ohio, and the Harlem Children Zone in New York. I personally commend these schools for the exceptional work they have done in producing positive measurable outcomes for boys of color. These educational models provide a blueprint for future practitioners who desire to affect change in the lives of Black boys. Let's keep the dream alive!

---

1. Fast Facts, Web.
2. Definition of Pedagogy in English, Web.
3. What Is Asperger's Syndrome? Symptoms, Tests, Causes, Treatments, Web.
4. ADHD Testing Issues regarding Testing, Drugging, and Diagnosis of ADD/ADHD, Web.
5. Gap Between Black and White Male High School Graduation Rates Still Widening, Web.
6. Qiu, Web.
7. Boser, Web.
8. Matheson, Kathy, Web.

Reflective Questions

1. What are some ways teachers can differentiate their instruction to keep Black boys engaged in the learning process?

_____
_____
_____
_____
_____
_____

2. Why do you suppose coaches have more success with Black boys than classroom teachers?

_____
_____
_____
_____
_____
_____

3. List your son's favorite teacher and coach. Ask these individuals if they would be willing to serve as a mentor for your son.

_____
_____
_____
_____
_____
_____

Don't Make Assumptions

It is back to school time. Summer vacation is over and a new school year is underway. Teachers are returning back to work early to decorate their classrooms and prepare for a new batch of learners. Rejuvenated from having had the summer off, they eagerly anticipate their students' arrival. Hosting back to school nights, shaking parent's hands, explaining curriculums, exhibiting warm demeanors, welcoming any questions parents may have, and extending an invitation to be contacted if any questions or concerns should arise is primary on their "To do List." But how long will it be before these same teachers begin gossiping about their problem students and discontentment with the administration in the Teacher Lounge?

Sadly, this is a bonding ritual that takes place across grade levels in most public school buildings. Teachers gossiping about their students have become an educational pastime. They might forget to record grades or complete student lesson plans, but they remember and discuss everything their "problem students" did with perfect clarity. From the moment a boy misbehaves, he becomes a target for his homeroom teacher and every teacher with whom she gossips to in the hallway and on the telephone. In fact, his teacher will wait and observe his every move with laser like precision in hopes that he will do something worthy of an office referral so she can have him removed from her classroom. Truth be told, he didn't have a chance at redemption because his teacher wrote him off when he committed his first offense. In her mind, boys that look like him are bad and don't deserve a second chance.

Don't Make Assumptions

From a cultural standpoint you would expect white teachers to be more understanding and empathetic toward children with whom they can relate to; children who look like them and share similar features as their own children, nieces, and nephews. This makes perfect sense if we look at it objectively. After all, relationships are the result of people being able to relate to one another, which explains why we have division and isolation between membership groups. People feel more comfortable being around members of their own race, religion, or political group. Society conditions us from childhood to process our surroundings in terms of race and ethnicity, sexual orientation, and socioeconomic status. Just about every document requiring your personal information asks for your sex, race, and ethnicity. The system at work in America forces us to identify ourselves based on some membership group. Requirements like these demonstrate the hypocrisy in our pledge of allegiance. There is no one nation under God, indivisible with liberty and justice for all. Having to label oneself by membership group, especially racial group creates a divided America. So for teachers to see Black boys as a different group from their White students is as natural for them as breathing.

It is perfectly understandable that teachers would feel more comfortable interacting with students who are familiar. Apprehension occurs when situations force them to chart unfamiliar territory. This is exactly what plays out in the classroom: young White teachers unable to connect with Black boys because they cannot relate to them culturally or socially. These boys are polar opposites of what they're used to, and because society demonizes Black boys, teachers feel justified in having them placed in a more restrictive setting. This is a perfect example of how cultural incompetence negatively impact student academic and behavioral outcomes. There is, however, despite these disparities, an opportunity to correct these prejudgments about Black boys if groups would be willing to look past individual differences and embrace the fact that there is a common thread we all share that transcends race and ethnicity. The challenge, however, would be getting groups to accept that we are not races and ethnicities, but spirit beings made in the image of an invisible Creator. In truth, we are one.

Don't Make Assumptions

Although Black boys act out in ways that may be different from students living in middle class neighborhoods, it does not negate the fact that they are the product of infinite intelligence and as such have the capacity to learn. Admittedly, a lot of our Black boys can be loud and exhibit behaviors that teachers may find physically intimidating; those behaviors are simply defense mechanisms. It is simply how they express themselves and hide their personal shortcomings. They simply need to be retaught and introduced to proper social norms. Behind that rough and tough exterior are vulnerable children in need of direction and support from caring adults. Teachers would do well to understand these defensive strategies and why Black boys exercise them. Not every child comes to school with the knowledge of middle class values ready to learn. This is an untested assumption that a lot of middle class White teachers make.

This assumption gives rise to the belief that every child will sit quietly, raise their hands before interjecting, walk in a straight line, and say yes mam and no mam and yes sir and no sir. How absurd. It is unfair for any teacher to make such an untested assumption and hold students accountable to a set of expectations that no adult has taken time to teach them. Students come to school with the best manners they have. Many of their parents are unfamiliar with middle class values. Therefore, they can't teach what they don't know. So what do we do? Do we throw the baby out with the bath water or do we roll up our sleeves and teach? If you are a teacher, you teach. Degrees and licenses do not make you a teacher. The fact that you teach makes you a teacher.

Good teachers understand that a learning deficiency implies a lack of instruction and takes advantage of this deficit as an opportunity to impart instruction. What kind of teacher are you? I am not suggesting that teachers make excuses for children displaying bad manners. I am, however, suggesting that teachers take the time to teach classroom norms and explain the role that rules play in creating and preserving order inside the classroom. As my college professor once said, "*Rules without relationship equals rebellion.*" It is not enough for teachers to say to a child "do this" or "do that" without explaining why the child should do "this" or "that." How a lesson relates to the classroom environment or life in general must precede rigor or students will not grasp the objectives of the lesson. A connection must be made.

Another major strategy to improve relationships between Black boys and White teachers is colleges and universities incorporating cultural competency courses into their teaching programs. This will better equip young White teachers to interact with and instruct students who come to school from low socioeconomic backgrounds with a different set of values. These courses should focus on non-punitive strategies that help schools reduce short and long-term suspensions and special education placements for behavioral disorders. This knowledge would position teachers to better understand their Black male students, while also reducing office referrals and the number of students referred for psychological evaluations. Utilizing this strategy would demonstrate a commitment to doing what's best for children rather than relying on quick fixes. As research constantly confirms, quick fixes are not in the best interest of children.

Of equal importance to this teacher to student relationship between White teachers and Black boys is the issue of "non-academic barriers" or non-school related issues that directly impact a student's ability to learn. For example, if a child comes to school hungry, tired, dirty, or abused, how attentive will he be to story time or learning his multiplication facts? How favorably will he respond to a sarcastic or condescending teacher who embarrasses him in front of his peers? Or what about the homeless boy living in his family's car or the boy selling drugs to help his single mother put food on the table? How can teachers, having not advocated for these boys, hold them accountable to the same standards as their more stable peers? Teachers need to take a moment out of their busy day and peer over their rose-colored lenses and take in the world from the perspective of their students. The view just might change an office referral to a hug and a conversation.

Don't Make Assumptions

Teachers who are passionate about children must make every effort to support Black boys before giving up on them. Schools can't become comfortable with having these boys tested, suspended, and expelled lest we leave an entire group of children behind. I challenge teachers and administrators to take the difficult road of extending themselves to help these children. I know it's easy to refer boys for testing, suspend them, and have them arrested for minor infractions, but taking the time to ask the simple question "Is everything alright?" Or "What's wrong?" could be the difference between a suspension and building a trust relationship with a boy in need.

As adults, we must communicate through our actions that we are genuinely interested in and committed to our children's betterment. And while I wish our children were savvier in how they reacted to a teacher's mistreatment, the ownership for modeling appropriate behavior should start with teachers not students. If adults want respect, they must be willing to conduct themselves in a respectable manner. In other words, adults should model the expectations. Yelling at a student in the hallway because he is not walking in a straight line says you are just as unsophisticated in your thinking process as the child. I can understand a kindergartner acting out, but how do you explain a college educated teacher throwing a temper tantrum because she can't manage the behavior of a five year old? Take a moment and really think about that.

Sometimes children act out inappropriately because acting out is the only way they know how to get an adult's attention. They use behavior as an attention-seeking vehicle. Each of us wants to be noticed and validated. I don't know anyone who is not concerned about feeling valued. Our Black boys literally fight for this approval. The need to be accepted is something that is inherent. I can't imagine any boy waking up thinking, "Today I think I will drop out of school and become a drug dealer or a gang banger." These choices are the result of him having experienced failure in some public school. How many out of school suspensions and F's does he have to see on his report card before the message, "I am not smart enough to be in school" or

"I don't belong here," becomes his reality? With him feeling incompetent and inadequate, it is only a matter of time before he turns to the street life to access the approval he didn't receive from school. If teachers do not get this, we will continue to see the dropout rate escalate for Black boys in America.

It is our responsibility as parents and teachers to provide Black boys with the necessary resources they need to succeed in public schools. This requires a comprehensive planning process that addresses their needs across home, school, and community. It means everyone coming to the table, committing their time, talents, and treasure, to expand the services of local schools in meeting the needs of their most challenged students. By comprehensive planning, I mean an interdisciplinary team of formal and informal service providers coming together to plan for children holistically. A team-based effort like this expands the school's resources and creates an environment where all students have what they need to perform well. This in my opinion is just and fair. And while I know it is a lot to ask underpaid and overworked school staff to participate on additional teams, think about the results that could be achieved if interdisciplinary teams used data to collectively plan on how to best utilize resources to improve academic and behavioral outcomes for its Black male student population.

Coming together creating a real educative community would be mirror the efforts of 9/11 when the country mobilized its resources to address an issue that threatened national security. Communities did not assume that New York City would be okay. I can't recall any agency labeling that tragedy a "New York problem" or refusing to allocate its resources because it would overextend their budget. America acted collectively because there was a city that needed our immediate assistance. Just think of the possibilities if formal service providers and community-based agencies embraced a similar mindset. Racial disparities would disappear because agencies committed their resources and energy until the problem was solved. This is something that every person reading this book should contemplate and aspire to accomplishing. Will you be a part of making this a realistic goal?

Reflective Questions

1. List the non-academic barriers that impact your son's ability to learn. Contact the school support staff to discuss your findings and concerns.

_____
_____
_____
_____
_____
_____

2. List your son's favorite teacher, coach, pastor, neighbor, relative etc. Invite them to all school meetings to serve as advocates for your son.

_____
_____
_____
_____
_____
_____

3. Make having dinner around the table a family ritual so your son can share his day and school issues. Write down and discuss his concerns.

_____
_____
_____
_____
_____
_____

Tribute to Hip Hop

Beef: and unsettled grief because a nigger was spitting hate through his teeth and the only recourse was to have that brother rest in peace. Unresolved conflict, unfair splitting of the profit, boys riding deep to handle it over some he said she said bullshit. Rappers seeking retaliation because of what they heard on a radio station; bulletproof vests and loaded heaters to settle what someone said across subwoofers and tweeters. How many bodies have to drop, from the "pop-pop-pop" of a nine or a Glock before the beefing finally stops? Because the impact of a hot track can destroy lifelong contacts; causing boys unite and ultimately fight against another crew for the lyrics they recite, while using the mic to viciously ignite a fire that's only quenched at the burial site. I hope and pray for that glorious day when the beefing comes to an end and the spirit of Hip Hop reunite those that use to be friends!

Focus On The Strengths

Hip Hop has become the voice of a generation. Like the free love of the 60's and the Black Power movement of the 70's, Hip Hop is the grassroots movement of the inner-city. For as long as I can remember, this particular genre of music has been providing young people with a platform to express their social and political views. This rings true for disenfranchised Black boys residing in America's urban neighborhoods. Hip Hop has given them someone to emulate, someone who looks like them and talks and walks like them. It packages and presents their reality in the realist and most celebratory manner. I personally love Hip Hop. Not that I embrace the use of the word "Nigger" or "Bitch," or the glorifying of Black on Black violence. For me, Hip Hop has always been a vehicle for Black people to orally paint their reality on digital canvas. More than rhyming schemes and funky beats, Hip Hop embodies and gives voice to the struggles of Black boys who share many of the experiences and live in similar hoods as the emcees shouting across the microphone.

Many, I am sure, will agree that when Public Enemy released *"Fight the Power"* it brought about a sense of racial consciousness among Black youth. This militant rap group gave boys from around the way a voice to speak out against the disparities and inequities in White America. It related to the disenfranchised, providing a stage for street lyricists to voice their dissatisfaction with the system. Just listen to the lyrical flow of emcees skillfully spitting across the microphone incorporating rhyme and meter, grammar and syntax, mastering the mechanics of a language arts curriculum. Not even the public school system, with its Common Core standards, academic textbooks, and licensed professional teachers can excite students to write about social, political, and economic issues with such fervor as Hip

Hop. This genre of music embraces our boys with a "non-blaming, non-judgmental attitude" building on their strengths and encouraging them to embrace their unique learning style.

As a movement Hip Hop has created a culture that glorifies the hood life. If your family is poor and dysfunctional and the school system and penal institutions have targeted your son, Hip Hop has a platform for him to tell his story. It does not look at him in disdain because he is sagging. Not that I am an advocate of our boys wearing their pants below their waist. I think sagging is more about self-esteem than dress code. When I look at our boys and see the hardness and anger on their faces, it pierces me to my soul causing me to wonder, "Why are these boys so angry and comfortable wearing their pants off their behind? Where is the pride in their appearance? What would make them feel comfortable looking so down trodden and scruffy? After long consideration, the answer came to me so inspiringly.

A boy's teenage years are supposed to be the memorable and enjoyable years of his life. When I was in school everything was about looking good. My peers and I wore Kangol hats with colored Lee jeans, name belts, and Adidas with no strings. This is how we attracted the pretty girls. Those were the golden years of my life and I remember them with perfect clarity, but the same is not true for this generation. In thinking about our boys' plight, I often ask myself, "How would I feel if I was poor, uneducated, and fatherless, with no real chance at a productive future? What would my mindset be? How would I feel if a good education was out of my grasp because those responsible for educating me, despised and rejected me? Would I come to school dressed for success ready to learn or would I feel resentful and angry? If in fact that were my state of mind, would I care what others thought about my style of dress? Would I even respect or acknowledge their opinion or feel a sense of guilt for taking their last breath?" These are the things I have pondered resulting in me not casting judgment, but rather seeking to heal and to help. Yes, sagging pants is an unsavory trend, but I see it as a reflection of how our boys feel inside. If you don't like yourself, how can you respect yourself? This is an important fact that should not be overlooked.

The Merriam-Webster Dictionary defines respect as valuing or holding something in high regard. Now I ask you, who has made our boys feel deserving of high regard? Is it the teacher who would rather write a referral for minor infractions than utilize behavioral strategies to keep him in her classroom, or is it the punitive-minded administrator who wholeheartedly embraces the belief that the pen is mightier than the sword? In which of these two scenarios, have Black boys been made to feel accepted and approved? Can you really expect students that schools have made to feel unintelligent and behaviorally inappropriate to feel valued and worthy of high regard? I can understand why these boys' pants are down. It is their way of saying to the spectators and naysayers "Kiss my black ass!" Admittedly, this sounds harsh, but based on the mistreatment of this population, it is definitely warranted. Who wants to be in a place where they feel unwanted and devalued? And while teachers may not say it directly, their yelling and impatience, and referrals for psychological testing, clearly demonstrate their disdain for Black boys. This is why our boys gravitate to the street life.

Children want to be around people who are accepting of them. It is imperative that school systems understand this. You can't label a boy unintelligent, a behavior problem, and advocate for him to be prescribed psychiatric medication and then expect him to be excited about learning. What sane person would voluntarily spend time in an environment that consistently magnified their deficits and pathology and minimized their strengths and capabilities? Focusing on a child's deficits only creates barriers to building a trusting relationship. While members of the medical community and public school system accept Attention Deficit Disorder (ADD) and Attention Deficit Hyperactivity Disorder (ADHD) as valid diagnoses, there are no medical tests to validate these disorders. The American Psychiatric Association voted this disorder into existence by a majority vote of its members.[1] If you take a look in the DSM V, you will note that the characteristics of ADD and ADHD are typical of normal child behavior. Judge for yourself:

Inattentiveness:

- Often fails to give close attention to details or makes careless mistakes in schoolwork, at work, or with other activities.

- Often has trouble holding attention on tasks or play activities.

- Often does not seem to listen when spoken to directly.

- Often does not follow through on instructions and fails to finish schoolwork, chores, or duties in the workplace (e.g., loses focus, side-tracked).

- Often has trouble organizing tasks and activities.

- Often avoids, dislikes, or is reluctant to do tasks that require mental effort over a long period of time (such as schoolwork or homework).

- Often loses things necessary for tasks and activities (e.g. school materials, pencils, books, tools, wallets, keys, paperwork, eyeglasses, mobile telephones).

- Is often easily distracted

- Is often forgetful in daily activities.

  Hyperactivity/Impulsivity:

- Often fidgets with or taps hands or feet, or squirms in seat.

- Often leaves seat in situations when remaining seated is expected.

- Often runs about or climbs in situations where it is not appropriate (adolescents or adults may be limited to feeling restless).

- Often unable to play or take part in leisure activities quietly.

- Is often "on the go" acting as if "driven by a motor."

- Often talks excessively.

- Often blurts out an answer before a question has been completed.

- Often has trouble waiting his/her turn.

- Often interrupts or intrudes on others (e.g., butts into conversations or games).[2]

Each of these characteristics are not only typical of children, but subjective, which means the results will vary depending on who is observing the child and how he or she defines the word "often." The question I have concerning this process is, what if the person making a determination between what is normal and abnormal has a racial bias? How can parents be certain that prejudice isn't tainting the process? There is no medical test to substantiate these two disorders.

The National Institute of Health Consensus Conference on ADHD, has also reported that there is no independent, valid test for ADHD, and there is no evidence linking ADHD to brain malfunction. Despite this lack of evidence for establishing ADHD as a mental illness, doctors are prescribing students drugs that the U.S. Drug Enforcement Administration place in the same class as highly addictive substances such as cocaine, morphine, and opium. Even the American Psychiatric Association, American Medical Association, and the National Institute of Mental Health have concluded the same thing: there are no medical tests to confirm mental disorders as a disease! It is so important that before you agree to having doctors prescribe psychiatric drugs to your son, ask the doctor for the lab results, blood tests, or X-ray confirming his diagnosis.[3] Doctors diagnose children with ADHD based on interviews with the parents, relatives, teachers, or other adults, who personally observe the child, questionnaires or rating scales that measure ADHD symptoms, and psychological tests.[4] This in no way justifies placing a child on addictive substances.

The truth is that ADHD and the prescribing of medication is about profiting off Black boys. As a matter of fact, a recent article revealed that, "More Ritalin is consumed in the United States than in all the other countries of the world combined. North America accounts for about 96 percent of the world's Ritalin consumption."[5] The number of students served under IDEA legislation has grown at nearly twice the rate of the general education population. Between the years 1980 to 2005, the IDEA student population has increased by 37 percent in comparison to the general education population that has grown by only 20 percent.[6] Here is where an informed parent becomes the best advocate for his or her son. Knowing your rights as a parent, especially as it pertains to his education, will position you to be your son's biggest advocate.

As advocates for their sons, every parent should know their rights. One basic right that every parent should be familiar with is the fact that no school receiving federal dollars can deny your son an education because you refuse to have him placed on medication. Congress made this amendment to the Individuals with Disabilities in Education Act (IDEA) in 2004. It included a section that prohibited "mandatory medication" in schools. The Act specifically states that, *"The State educational agency shall prohibit State and local educational agency personnel from requiring a child to obtain a prescription for a substance covered by the Controlled Substances Act (21 U.S.C. 801 et seq.) as a condition of attending school…"*[7] This only makes sense. The symptoms of ADD and ADHD are typical of any energetic child. Black boys are naturally energetic, so sitting through hours of boring content is contrary to their nature. I find it quite interesting, however, that these same boys described as inattentive and hyperactive can sit through a 2-hour movie, a 3-hour church service, and hours of videogames, Snapchat, YouTube, and Instagram. This is proof that interesting content can keep them engaged and connected.

As an After-School Specialist, I personally witnessed boys playing games that required sophisticated mathematical and reading skills for hours on end without a staff member having to redirect them. Likewise, I have witnessed other boys glued in front of Sony Play Stations and laptop computers focusing for hours, undistracted by whatever else was going on in the room. Attention span, considering this evidence, cannot be the problem since it only manifests in classrooms where culturally incompetent teachers force-feed hours of boring content. Many of these teachers' present information in such a dry uninteresting manner that our boys express their disinterest in the only manner they know how: they tune out, daydream, or become restless and fidgety! This is the same as the teacher who doodles on her PowerPoint handout, holds sidebar conversations with the person seated next to her, and texts underneath the table. Again I ask, is it really an Attention Deficit Disorder or the inability to focus on boring content?

It is the same with Attention Deficit Hyperactivity Disorder (ADHD). Why is having to move around and engage others considered a disorder? Movement is natural. As adults, we exercise our autonomy to move around at our leisure, but we limit students to their seat. Children do not have the luxury of standing up to stretch their legs during a lesson. If they lack the ability to sit through a class period, teachers are quick to refer them for testing. This is nothing short of hypocrisy. The fact that a child wants to do something other than sleep in class has to account for something. Teachers should use this energy and need for movement to their advantage before seeking the quick fix of testing and medication. Every teacher should espouse to the core value that all children can and want to learn. It is unfortunate that many of the teachers instructing Black boys, at present, do not prescribe to this guiding principle. Every child is different so it is unrealistic to believe that all students will learn the same way. Differentiation should be a part of any institution made up of diverse student populations. Why then, are teachers delivering information in a manner that has proven ineffective for their Black male students? An acronym suitable for this teaching disorder should be DDD (Differentiation Deficit Disorder).

As I stated earlier, the streets have created an environment conducive for making our boys feel valued. The streets give them an opportunity to be productive using their natural skill set. In the streets our boys have a strong reputation. They have knocked out other boys in street battles, manufactured and sold large quantities of street drugs for a profit, and bedded some of the prettiest girls in their neighborhood. The streets applaud their achievements. This, however, is not what happens to these young honorees once they enter the school building.

At school these boys are labeled a disruption, behavior problem, or a diagnosis and pathology that teachers are forced to deal with because of mandatory attendance laws. This is a recipe for academic failure and increased dropout rates. Every child wants to feel normal. If they are in a place that makes them feel abnormal, the typical response is to avoid that environment. Why do school folk think it strange when students exhibit a typical response? Why would a child feel excited about spending time in an environment that depicts him as incompetent and unmanageable when he can hang out in the streets and feel a sense of pride and acceptance? This is not rocket science. Instead of focusing on the deficits of these boys, which our schools and doctors are all too quick to do, we should be focusing on and developing their talents and strengths. These boys are excellent entrepreneurs and communicators. They tend to do poorly in school because classrooms are not designed for left brained kinesthetic learners.

This was the case with my son Brandon. Over time he developed a strong dislike for school. Not that he hated learning—he hated the way his teachers delivered their instruction. I noticed, however, that Brandon and his earphones were inseparable. Every morning during the drive to school, he would have his IPod on. Then one morning like Oprah, I experienced an "Aha" moment. "Why am I trying to reinvent the wheel, I asked myself?"

"Brandon is not a traditional learner. His learning style was more auditory and kinesthetic. He could recite the latest rap lyrics without missing a single word. This was a clear indicator that music and technology were the tools I needed to get him excited about learning.

That night I called Brandon downstairs and asked him, *"How would you feel if your teachers let you use your cell phone to record class lectures? You could record your test reviews or videotape the steps to solving difficult math equations and play it over and over again until you were able to recite it just like your favorite rap song. Do you think the use of technology would encourage you take a more active approach to studying? You could learn the same information, but in a different way. Unlike the traditional method of reading pages and pages of print, you could listen to the information."* The idea of an alternative to reading pages and pages of content appealed to Brandon. Reading was something he usually did to maintain his cell phone and IPad2 privileges, but he'd listen to music hours on end without me threatening him.

I have since come to appreciate that as parents we have to use whatever works to advance our Black boys. This means taking advantage of the latest technology. Technology works and our kids love it. How many students are on Facebook, YouTube, Instagram, and Snapchat? Kids spend countless numbers of hours on the Internet. Why then, aren't teachers using technology and social media as educational resources? Why aren't they using smart phones, iPads, and social media sites since these are the resources monopolizing our boys' attention? I know this is a radical shift in our educational paradigm, but we are living in a technological world and the educational model that worked for our parents and grandparents is failing to graduate our boys from high school and equip them with the necessary skills to be competitive at a local and national level.

Our current educational system is in a state of crisis as evidenced by the dropout rates for Black males. America's refusal to reduce its reliance on punitive strategies and embrace a new way of reaching and teaching its Black male students is killing their dreams. The system must either change or die. If public school systems expect to be successful in educating Black boys, the system is going to have to be flexible in its approach and make education both relevant and rigorous, by utilizing technologies that kids naturally gravitate toward. If it works and it is good for children, why are schools discouraging the use of it? Prohibiting the use of smartphones in a learning institution is not smart on the school's behalf. The mission of any school system should be to educate all of its students. Right? So why then are schools refusing to embrace every resource at their disposal to accomplish its mission? Technology is simply a vehicle for mobilizing students from daily attendance to graduation.

Employing the use of technology encourages students to take ownership for their learning. It makes the learning process relevant and engaging. Imagine a classroom where students are in charge of setting up video equipment, recording classroom instruction, editing video content, uploading media files, and serving as the systems administrator for the class blog. An environment like this inspires student learning because it uses the very things our boys connect with. It also encourages their active participation. This is true education and kinesthetic learners will love these activities.

Another way for teachers to incorporate technology as a way of making the learning process relevant with current content is to have students create class Wiki pages. Wiki pages are pages that interlink information from various websites making it readily available and easily accessible to the viewer. This is a great way for teachers to inform parents and the community about class schedules, school events, lesson plans, student portfolios, and volunteer opportunities. It is a way to move education into the 21st century. Embracing this kind of "whatever works approach" provides both teachers and students the freedom and flexibility to improve academic outcomes for all children. I encourage every school to rethink their policies on the use of cell phones and social media in the classroom. It could result in improved student academic outcomes.

So I say to the public school system, let the artist learn math through drawing, let the singer learn language arts through writing and song lyrics, and let the dancer learn history by acting out his rendition of major events. More importantly, let children learn by pulling out what is naturally within them. Again I say, let the children learn!

---

1. Eakman, Web.
2. Rabiner, Web.
3. Parents: Get the Facts—Know Your Rights, Web.
4. Bhandari, Web.
5. DeGrandpre and Hinshaw, Web.
6. Individuals With Disabilities Act Cost Impact On Local School Districts, Web.
7. Prohibition on Mandatory Medication, Web.

Reflective Questions

1. What way best describes how your son learns new information: watching videos, listening to music, reading a book, or by hands-on? Share this information with his teachers.

_____
_____
_____
_____
_____
_____

2. Make a list of all your son's technological devices (e.g., iPad, iPod, iPhone, laptop, Kindle, desktop computer etc.)

_____
_____
_____
_____
_____
_____

3. How can he use these devices to improve his performance in school?

_____
_____
_____
_____
_____
_____

Where is my Father?

Where is my father? Has anyone seen him or am I simply the end result of two people too irresponsible to use birth control? Damn, it's hard not to be angry when you can't explain why your father doesn't want to see you. Where is my father? Has anyone spoken to him? I only know his name because I read it on my birth certificate and it didn't even match my last name. Momma kept a wrinkled picture of him in her purse but she never showed it to me. My grandmother told me the man in the picture was my father. Where is my father grandma? I need him in my life. He was supposed to teach me how to be a man. Grandma just hugged me and said, I know baby, I know. It hurts like hell because I always felt it was my fault that he wasn't there. Maybe I wasn't good enough to deserve his attention or affection. My mother tried to care for me but she was addicted to having to have a man in her life. Maybe her having been with different men explains why my brothers and sisters don't look like me and why each of them gets to go places on Saturdays with men who seem happy to see them. I long for someone to look at me like that but momma says I'm the bad child. She says I'm just like my father and won't amount to anything. My teachers look at me the same way momma does. They always send me out of their class to the Principal's office. I guess momma and the teachers are right about me. Where is my father, Mr. Principal? Have you seen him? I need to talk to him because the judge says I am headed down the wrong road. He says I shouldn't have to work to buy my school clothes, especially if it means late nights on the corner looking out for the police. Momma is still telling me that I am going to end up just like my father. I hear her crying at night when I come in late from the streets. One night while momma is crying, men in blue uniforms pick me up and take me to a new home. I no longer have to ask, "Where is my father?" I know where my father is now as I am given an orange jumpsuit just like the one he wore in the picture. Somehow, I believe that fate will allow our paths to cross as momma's words of me being just like my father are fulfilled. I wish we didn't have to meet like this.

Part 3:
What Parents Can Do

Knowledge of Self

The book of Proverbs explicitly states that you are what you think (Proverbs 23:7). Thoughts are the things that create our reality. This means that whatever your son thinks about the most, will eventually manifest as his truth. Therefore, the questions that each parent must answer are these: What is the reality of a boy who perceives himself as academically inferior and behaviorally inappropriate because school systems have labeled, medicated, and placed him in a self-contained environment? What is the likelihood he will aspire to a four-year college or university and become a future leader in America? Research says that his chances are slim to none. So what can you as a parent do to change his thinking process? Training your son on his history and helping him develop a strong sense of self is key to both his mental and social advancement.

Knowledge of self is the vehicle that mobilizes a people from darkness to an elevated state of enlightenment. Therefore, it is important for our sons to learn about the African men who invented science, mathematics, and writing systems. It is equally important that they learn about the origin of religion and mystery schools and their beginnings on the continent of Africa. This information alone can be life changing and will inspire our boys to greatness! It will give them a sense of pride in their black skin and African heritage. Teaching them about their African ancestors has got to become the duty of every Person of Color. By ancestors, I referencing people other than those linked to chattel slavery and the civil rights movement. From my experience, restricting their exposure to these historical figures will only create resentment and hatred for White folks and contempt for their skin color and black features. That is why we witness Black boys playing the dozens, cracking on how black another boy is or how nappy his hair is. In their mind being black is a deficit because of how society portrays People of Color.

While I appreciate the bravery of the Black slaves and civil rights leaders who sacrificed their lives for me, our boys need to have a frame of reference linking them to something other than subservience and segregation. If we as a people only expose our boys to Black people in menial roles looking to their White slave masters for basic inalienable rights, it will make them feel mentally inferior to White folks. It will freeze them in a time in history when White folks owned their ancestors. Such a limited frame of reference can't possibly make our boys feel equal to their White counterparts. They need to know who their ancestors were before they were enslaved in America. They need to learn about great black men like Amenhotep, Akhenaten, and Tutankhamen. These men walked the planet as gods, shaping and designing what we have come to appreciate as Western civilization.

So we must ask ourselves, why are Black boys failing in subjects that men of color not only created, but also mastered? Why are our boys not proficient in reading and math on end of year tests? These potential young scholars need to know that it was men of African descent that gave the world its vast body of knowledge. They need to know that great philosophers like Socrates, Plato, and Aristotle obtained their knowledge from books that the Greeks stole from the Alexandrian Library in Egypt.[1] That little bit of information could be life changing for a boy who equates intelligence with white faces.

Think for a moment about how powerful we would be as a people if the sororities and fraternities of our Historically Black Colleges and Universities came to understand that the initiation process and the secret knowledge to which they affirm is rooted in Egyptian mystery schools. How would this information impact our college educated brothers and sisters if they understood the African origins of these groups? Would it cause them to embrace Africa the way they do Greece? Or what would happen if our

Black college students came to realize that the Greeks actually stole their knowledge from the Africans during the conquests of Alexander the Great? What would happen if they came to learn that every race on the planet originated with an Ethiopian woman who lived over 200,000 years ago?[2] How would that knowledge impact the displaced African in America who thinks that being Greek is something to celebrate?

These are the things that Black boys need to hear if we expect to develop a race of young scholars who have a sincere appreciation for their African origins and confidence in their intellectual capacity. Public schools are not going to teach these kinds of lessons. This is where parents and grandparents are instrumental. Exposing our boys to their African origins has to become a family affair. If a book affirms the greatness of African people, expose your son to it and then teach it to every Black boy in your family, neighborhood, and church! Our goal is to transform the collective thinking and behavior of Black boys. For our boys to develop a basic knowledge about Africa and its contribution to the disciplines of math, science, and politics would have a positive impact on how they see themselves. This is a primary step in reducing the self-hatred that results in Black on Black homicide. We must not deprive our boys of this opportunity to feel a sense of historical accomplishment and self-pride. My question to you, mom and dad, is what will your first lesson be?

---

1. James, Web.
2. Cann, pg. 30-37.

Reflective Questions

1. List 3 affirmations your son can recite every morning.

_____
_____
_____
_____
_____
_____

2. What are some contributions that Africans have made to Western civilization? Complete this project with your son.

_____
_____
_____
_____
_____
_____

3. Have your son make a list of his physical features (lips, nose, hair etc.). Next to each physical feature, have him write down the characteristics of dominant genes for each feature. Discuss why "dominant" genes are superior to "recessive" genes to help him develop a positive self-image.

_____
_____
_____
_____
_____
_____

Bestow The Blessing

Lincoln's signing of the emancipation proclamation may have legally freed the slaves, but it did not make up for White slave masters and their offspring's four hundred year head start in the race for social advancement. The question then must be asked, How can America in good conscience, negate giving reparations to a people whose ancestors they stripped of their names, language, and religion—the very things that establish a peoples cultural identity? For emancipated slaves to have to establish their own cultural identity, learn to read and write, and compete for resources in an economy that your formers owners created without monetary reparations is not only unfair, but unrealistic. What happened to our 40-acres and a mule?

As a defense against giving reparations to the descendants of African slaves, white conservatives will more often than not reference how other cultures migrated to America and were successful in obtaining the American Dream. What they fail to mention in their argument is the voluntary nature in which those other races and ethnicities came to this country and the culture and history they brought along with them. Negro slaves are the only people arriving on American soil not in search of the American Dream. Slaves were the recipients of the American nightmare. It was their toil and sweat that created the American Dream. The slave received nothing in exchange for his labor, not even a minimum wage. Think about the dollar amount America owes the Negro for his years of involuntary servitude. No one can dispute the fact that every dream received by the people of this great melting pot nation has been afforded to them by the sweat equity of the Negro slaves. To this day, the offspring of these emancipated slaves are still awaiting some form of payment for their forefathers labor, so please don't insult me by playing the "other immigrants did it" card. Anything is possible when people know who they are and are, have the autonomy to create a system that benefits their own, and is afforded unlimited wealth without taxation. This not only establishes the then existing generation, but generations to come.

This is not true for generations whose forefathers had no resources to leave them. What provisions did America make for the African in this country who out of necessity is still seeking to recover from years of cultural and historical amnesia, while at the same time competing for resources against races whose mental faculties have remained intact? What do you prescribe for a people that have no knowledge of their history or cultural identity? How do you suppose they recover from four hundred years of intergenerational poverty to create a sense of collective economic empowerment? This is a legitimate question that requires our attention as People of Color if we hope to empower our sons. Who are we as a people? What common threads of truth do we share besides chattel slavery, segregation, and soul food? These are basic questions that establishes a group's identity.

Common for people who meet for the first time is the question of asking, "Where are you from?" I have had the pleasure of meeting Irish, Italians, Germans, and a host of other cultures having served in the military. Each group with whom I met had a surname, language, and culture that directly established their racial identity, but this is not the case for the emancipated African in America? What is his native tongue or place of origin? What were the traditions of his people? What religion did his people practice? This is what America stole from the African. I am sure that Thomas is not the surname of my ancestors. It more closely resembles the surname of the slave master who purchased my ancestors. In all honesty, I cannot tell you where my family originated from or what language they spoke or their tribal affiliation. So while America embraces and admires the tenacity of immigrants, it must be said of them that they arrived at these borders with their surname, culture, language, religion, and race and ethnicity intact. The African in America has not been afforded that luxury. He is still searching for an identity in post-slavery America, and if these other immigrant groups were in his shoes, how else would they fare in a racist society with no sense of identity, the inability to read and write, and no resources with which to establish their claim in the world? Welcome to the world inherited by freed Africans and their offspring.

These unfortunate set of circumstances have not changed in the 21st century. The American media has made the Negro out to be less than other racial groups. He is viewed by the public as a dangerous criminal with the social functioning and intelligence of a primate. This explains to a large extent why Black boys are so angry. If it is true that you are what you eat, what does a diet of racist teachers, academic failure, excessive suspensions, and placements in youth correctional facilities produce? What we are witnessing today is the result of boys not feeling valued by society. The emptiness created by this rejection has created a generation of forgotten children. America has failed to bestow the blessing of a favorable future upon its Black males, and as Genesis chapters 25-27 clearly points out, there is an inherent power in the blessing that exceeds anything material. There we read about the life of two brothers, Jacob and Esau and their striving to be accepted and approved of by their father. For the sake of explaining the power of the blessing, I will focus my attention on the eldest sibling Esau and why he preferred the blessing above his birthright.

It is imperative that we first take a look at the story within its cultural context. Esau, as the eldest son of Isaac, occupied a position of favor in the family. Within the Hebrew culture, it was customary for the eldest son to be the heir of his father's birthright. For those of you unfamiliar with the birthright, it represents a double portion of a father's inheritance. The eldest son received it because he was responsible for looking after his widowed mother and virgin sisters in addition to caring for his own family. Therefore, the birthright was used to preserve the family in the absence of the father. Esau was the heir of this right because of birth order, but what I want you to understand about the birthright is that it was "material" in nature. Let me demonstrate the relationship between the birthright and the blessing and how it relates to Black boys in America.

As we read further into the story, we find that Esau despised his birthright. He had little respect for his father's possessions and the prosperity he was to inherit as the eldest sibling. Important to note here is the fact that Esau's father Isaac had inherited a wealthy estate from his father Abraham, making him a very wealthy man. Esau was next in line to receive the greater portion of this estate. So why did he give up this entitlement to his younger sibling Jacob for a bowl of soup? A bowl of soup! Clearly, he did not value his father's possessions. Do you hear me parents? Esau had little respect for his father's wealth. That should speak volumes to those of you struggling to purchase your children expensive sneakers and jeans, but do very little to make them feel validated. Gifts are not your son's priority!

Esau despised his birthright. He was more concern with receiving his father's blessing. The blessing represented his father bestowing a favorable future upon his life. It was his daddy's stamp of approval on his life. It was his way of showing he valued his son. That is what our boys are craving. They are looking for their fathers to bestow a favorable future upon their life. Learning deficits and low socioeconomic status is the result of a father not having foresight for his son. As fathers we must have a vision for our sons and speak it directly into their heart every day until it becomes a part of their long-term memory and manifests through their thinking and behavior.

The story culminates with young Jacob stealing Esau's blessing by deceiving their father Isaac, while he was on his deathbed. Upon realizing what his younger brother had done, Esau vowed to murder Jacob. Here is where we witness the power of the blessing over the birthright. Isaac's material possessions meant little to his eldest son. What Esau wanted more than anything from his father was his acceptance and approval. This is powerful stuff! As parents we sacrifice and work long hours convincing ourselves that we are doing it to provide a better life for our children. The goal is for them to have a better life than we had. I totally understand that, but what most parents fail to understand is that children would rather have our support and validation than our things. Wealth fails in comparison to validation. Wealth is worth a bowl of soup, but your acceptance and approval is priceless.

The fact that our sons are left without the approval of a loving father has made them angry murderers of their brothers. Black on Black homicide is a continuation of the Esau and Jacob melodrama. Where are the Isaacs in our community to bestow favorable futures upon our devalued boys? Family courts can order fathers to pay child support, but what judge can order a father to validate his son? Mothers can love and nurture their sons, but how can women teach their sons to be something they are not? Rearing a son is man's work. Proverbs 3:1-2 states, *"My son, do not forget my law, but let your heart keep my commands; for length of days and long life and peace they will add to you."* Fathers are commanded to instruct their sons in the ways that bring forth peace and length of days so they will have a favorable future.

Fathers, you are commanded to spend time teaching your son and less time buying for your son. A good life is not about your son having the latest Jordan's. It's about him achieving a favorable future. You are the Pastor, Priest, and Shepherd of your family. Therefore, I admonish you to teach your sons about the importance of honoring his father and mother so that his life conforms to the words spoken from your lips. What he becomes in life should be the result of the words spoken by his father, who through wisdom and foresight envisioned a favorable future for his life. Bind that vision upon the table of his heart and in his mind. Rehearse it in his ears until it takes shape and becomes his reality. Thoughts become things. I challenge every father to bestow the blessing upon his son by speaking a favorable future in his ears every day. Below are some of the things my father passed on to me in a letter before he transitioned to the next life. I wanted to share them with you in hopes that they will bless you the way they have me:

- Your life is the result of decisions, good and bad, so learn from your mistakes.

- There is nothing wrong with a male crying and displaying emotions.

- Do not be lazy, develop a good work ethic.

- Always put aside some finances for a rainy day.

- When you don't know what to do and have to make a quick decision, rely on common sense.

- Always think safety.

- Take responsibility for your actions.

- Never let others have more influence over you than your parents.

- Remember to give of your substance, let your life be a blessing to others.

- Avoid people who are constantly getting into trouble.

- Forgive others when they wrong you.

- Avoid talking bad about other people.

- Try to love everybody.

- Teach your children everything you know about the world before they leave home.

- Never do harm to your family members. It is better to walk away.

- Always get a second opinion when making important decisions.

- Keep a spirit of gratitude and develop a personal relationship with God.

Reflective Questions

1. What is the difference between the Birthright and the Blessing?

_____
_____
_____
_____
_____
_____

2. Write down the favorable future you envision for your son. Speak this into his ear every morning.

_____
_____
_____
_____
_____
_____

3. List some of the wise sayings of the elders of your family. Pass them on to your son so he can benefit from their wisdom.

_____
_____
_____
_____
_____
_____

What Do We Do?

Can I think out loud, can I just for a moment separate myself from the crowd? I just need a little time to pray, so that I can find the right words to say. Because right now I am at a lost, my people have paid a great cost. Do we migrate back to Africa or do we protest to address the unrest that my people feel in their heart? Where do we start? Is it a matter of civil rights legislation or our refusal to experience integration in a nation that has proven unjust, despite our trust, that the system will do what is best for us and provide for all people equal treatment under the law? Which way do we turn, is this a lesson we must learn, do we stay in the house and watch it burn? Do we pray, do we stay, is this a black and white issue or are there some shades of grey? Do we ask God to heal when we are the subjects of ill will? Do we as revolutionaries take up arms to kill? Did Marcus Garvey have it right? Did we miss our return flight? W.E.B. Dubois must not have known that the Negro would never be at home in the land of his captors, if only he could have had a preview of the upcoming chapters to see that the Negro would have no happily ever after.

Part 4:
What Communities Can Do

A Shared Vision For Change

"And the Lord answered me, and said, Write the vision, and make it plain upon tables..."
(Habakkuk 2:2)

The year was 2006, as the Executive Director of Reach One Teach One Academy Incorporated, I had to present before the local Juvenile Crime Prevention Council: a group responsible for reviewing the needs of juveniles and awarding agencies grant funding to provide community-based alternatives to incarceration for juvenile offenders. With only five minutes to convince the council members to fund my program, I stood passionately and addressed the members with these opening words:

"Good afternoon Council. I would first like to thank each member in his or her respective position for the opportunity to address this Council. Let me begin by saying, if I were an animal lover and the dolphins were becoming extinct, out of my concern for the dolphins, my conscience would force me to launch a "Save the Dolphins Campaign." Well, I am not an animal lover. I am, however, a youth advocate whose conscience has been greatly disturbed by the negative overrepresentation of black boys in special education and youth development centers. For that reason, I stand here before you this afternoon requesting funding to launch a Save the Black Boys' Campaign."

There is an African Proverb that states, *"It takes a village to raise a child."* Addressing racial disparities and creating a level playing field for Black boys is a matter that transcends any one agency or neighborhood. An issue of this magnitude calls for the employment of collective intelligence from an entire community. It requires the commitment of formal and informal agencies coming together discussing evidence-based strategies on how to best address the factors that place our sons at risk. From this conversation, groups must make a concerted effort to comprehensively plan for how to best implement these strategies across home, school, and community to improve the social and educational outcomes of Black boys. This in my opinion is a holistic approach to addressing the matter at hand. The bottom line is that if there is no village, we must create one.

In the early days of the New Testament church, we read in the book of The Acts of the Apostles about how the members of this grassroots nonprofit organized themselves to care for their members by donating their possessions to the common cause of removing poverty from amongst their membership. By creating a shared vision, this local movement built a community that created an equitable station of living for all their brothers and sisters. It took an entire village to bring about this change described in Acts 2:34: *"There was none among them that lacked."*

This is where I believe the Black church can play an active role in the process of reversing negative trends affecting Black boys. Churches can use their monetary resources to build our sons as an alternative to building brick and mortar. We must remember what the scriptures teach: The most High does not live in manmade buildings (Acts 7:48). With a Black church on every street corner in the United States, a person only has to take a moment to seriously consider how much change the church could create if they used their dollars to build lives opposed to religious buildings. Together Black churches could create change in threatened and fragile neighborhoods by building the true temple of God (1Corinthians 3:16).

It is my opinion that the Black church has to do more than meet for weekly services if they expect to see change in the Black boys who attend their services every Sunday. The civil rights movement, which centered on the bestowing of basic inalienable rights upon all Americans, produced some of the greatest results for Black folks in the history of this country. Like the church at Thessalonica, they turned the Roman Empire upside down (Acts 17:6). The church has the power and the opportunity to produce similar results in 21st century America. Jesus gave his followers their mission statement during his earthly ministry. The mission was to "Go" and make disciples so that a spiritual kingdom would operate on earth as it did in heaven (Matthew 28:19; Matthew 6:10). He understood that where a true spiritual kingdom operated, racism could not exist. Spiritual people are not defined nor are they restricted by race and ethnicity. They understand that love conquers all.

Just think of the national impact the Black church could have if Pastors put aside their egos and denominational differences to tackle the bigger issue of social injustice. Collectively, the church could bring about a national outcry and unification comparable to that of the civil rights era. And while I use the term Black church, there is only one church, but since Sunday morning is the most segregated hour in this country, I use the term to target those places of worship consisting of a large Black membership.[1] Religious racism, however, is a part of the social injustice that spiritual people must also tackle to improve the outcomes of Black males in America.

Under the Jim Crow, Black people actively engaged in acts of civil disobedience that brought about social and political change. This is the fervor that the Black church must duplicate as the light of the world and salt of the earth. It cannot afford to be indifferent toward social injustice. This is not the time to retreat inside a brick and mortar church building, while the big bad wolf of institutional racism huffs and puffs and blows poor communities down. Lives are at stake. It is high time for the church to make its presence known in the homes and streets of children that are being unfairly targeted by police and other governmental agencies including public school systems and juvenile justice agencies. This is not some farfetched idea. Change at this level can happen in the worst of circumstances as evidenced in the book of Nehemiah. There we read about how a group of disenfranchised Hebrews rebuilt the burned walls of Jerusalem by employing the collective intelligence and resources of their community.

A Shared Vision For Change

According to the Book of Nehemiah, a foreign enemy had invaded the city of Jerusalem and burned down its walls leaving it ruined in heaps of stones and ashes. The main character Nehemiah, upon hearing the report of the invasion from one of his Hebrew brothers, grew anxious knowing there were no walls to protect the city and fabric of Jewish life. This prompted him to yield himself as a willing vessel to be used by God to save the city. King Artaxerxes, Nehemiah's immediate supervisor and ruler of Persia, moved by Nehemiah's concern for his homeland, granted him a leave of absence from his place of employ to travel to Jerusalem where he functioned as the interim governor. Here is what I want you to grasp from the story.

Nehemiah was a Persian government official living in the palace of Shushan. He had excelled the political ladder, but his heart was still in Jerusalem. Repairing Jerusalem consumed him. Something had to be done to help his brothers from the old neighborhood. That's how I feel when I hear about the state of my young Black brothers. The fabric of the Black community has been burned with fire and our boys' hopes and dreams lay in ruin. There is no wall of defense to combat the invasion of curriculums of genocide, psychiatric drugs, and disproportionate minority contact in the juvenile justice system. We must organize ourselves as a racial group and rebuild our own communities. The condition of our sons' deserves our immediate attention.

The question now before us is, "Where do we begin?" What can we do at the grassroots level? Fortunate for us, we can mobilize our communities towards reaching a shared vision for change and a collective mission that defines our purpose, how we plan to accomplish that purpose, and for whom. It means that as a community, we must bring the right collaborative partners to the table and involve parents as equal partners in the planning process. This also means that we invite public school leaders to the table to discuss how a grassroots collaborative can help expand its array of services to address the non-academic barriers that negatively impact student outcomes.

A Shared Vision For Change

As a community of concerned citizens we must hold the Black church accountable and make sure it is giving of its resources to help rebuild our disenfranchised communities. If the community supports the Black church, then it is only right that the church shows up to support the Black community. It is estimated that Black people have $1 trillion in buying power and at least 60 percent of Black charitable dollars go to churches.[2] Studies also reveal that nearly two-thirds of Black households make charitable donations worth a total of about $11 billion a year.[3] It's only right, considering the amount of money donated by the Black community that the church give back to its supporters. From a practical perspective, the church should practice what it preaches. If members are expected to give a tenth of their income to the local church, we must demand the church allocate a tenth or tithe of what it receives to build our boys. Remember, the most High does not live in manmade church buildings (Acts 7:48). The kingdom of God is within us (Luke 17:21). Therefore, the church cannot possibly be a building. That alone should inform how the Black church allocates its funds. The goal should be to build people and ensure that none have lack. Is this how your local church allocates its dollars?

Another priority would be to facilitate partnerships between the local school system and Historically Black Colleges and Universities (HBCU) to provide training on cultural competence for White female teachers unfamiliar with the backgrounds of Black boys coming from economically disadvantaged neighborhoods. This is paramount to our boys' success and it will help address racial prejudice. The disconnect between White female teachers from middle class backgrounds whose sole orientation to teaching is college textbooks and lectures is a great divide that our HBCU'S can assist in bridging. Professional development that focuses on cultural competence can prepare White teachers to better understand and teach their low-income students. Remember, if teachers cannot RELATE to their students, how can they be expected to develop RELATIONSHIPS? Training is a practical strategy for challenging the notion that Black kids are bad.

A Shared Vision For Change

These are but a few of the action steps that People of Color and People of Concern can take if the goal is to create measurable and sustainable change. The only way we can change the condition of Black boys in America is to bring communities together so we can engage in a collective dialogue about our spiritual oneness. Then and only then will we eradicate race prejudice at its core when we embrace the fact that we, as spirit beings, simply occupy human bodies. Once we destroy race prejudice at its core, we can begin the tasks of creating a shared vision that includes fairness and equity for all races across all agencies. Then will the Negro truly be able proclaim those liberating words of Dr. King: Free at last, free at last, thank God almighty we are free at last! For then, we will have realized the Dream.

I have taken the liberty of summarizing the ideas presented in this book for a quick review. It is my hope that they will serve as a framework for creating change for our boys collectively:

1. The church must actively fulfill its mission of "Going" and making disciples so that the vision of creating a kingdom that operates on earth as it does in heaven becomes a reality. We must commit to creating a spiritual people not a race of people.

2. The church must practice a pure religion that cares for the spiritual, emotional, and educational needs of fatherless children.

3. We must begin changing our boys' behavior by renewing their minds, which means providing them with historical information that educates and empowers rather than depict them in menial and subservient roles.

4. We must teach our boys to become self-sufficient men as the Pastors, Providers, and Protectors of their home.

5. Fathers must speak a favorable future upon the lives of their sons so that it becomes ingrained in their mind and influence how they think and behave.

6. Fathers along with positive Black role models must teach our boys about financial literacy and entrepreneurship so we can mobilize the next generation forward from poverty to affluence.

7. Parents must keep their sons involved in positive activities with positive role models to divert them from negative behaviors.

8. Parents must advocate for their son's utilizing every formal and informal resource at their disposal to save their son from the destructive policies of systemic racism.

9. People of Color and People of Concern must come together and commit their time, talent, and treasure to providing interventions that address the non-academic barriers negatively impacting Black boys.

10. Partnerships must be developed between public school systems and HBCU'S to provide White teachers with professional training that addresses cultural competence and implicit bias.

11. Teachers must differentiate their instruction to meet the needs of their kinesthetic and tactile learners, while embracing the belief that every child can and will learn.

12. Schools must incorporate smart devices (phones, iPads, tablets etc.) into the classroom to connect what Black boys find relevant to the learning process.

13. Schools must convene interdisciplinary teams of formal and informal service providers to create and implement non-punitive strategies as alternatives to suspensions and arrests to reduce disproportionate minority contact in the juvenile justice system.

14. Schools along with their community partners must implement strategies that include parents and students as equal partners so that interventions are strength-based and meet the needs of Black boys across home, school, and community.

I am urging community-based nonprofits to contact their state educational agencies about Title IV-B 21st Century Community Learning Centers grant funds and their state Juvenile Justice agency about funding to reduce Disproportionate Minority Contact. Agencies can also contact their city's Workforce Development Board to inquire about Workforce and Innovation Opportunity Act (WIOA) funding. These dollars are allocated to states to improve student academic outcomes in the core content areas of reading and math and to provide community-based alternatives to secure detention and incarceration. WIOA dollars are allocated to help youth complete their high school education and gain entry in to college or the workforce.

Nonprofits, including faith-based agencies, are eligible to apply for these dollars in order to assist cities and states in their compliance with federal statutes. Change starts at the grassroots level. From my experience as a grant writer acquiring more than $21-million dollars for city, county, and nonprofit organizations, an interagency collaborative is best suited to apply for these dollars and implement the programs required under these funding sources. You can also contact me if your agency or community-based nonprofit is interested in discussing how to launch a community-based collaborative to address the racial disparities in your local community.

Reading this book is the first step toward change. The second and most challenging step is implementing the strategies. But as the Elders would say, "To whom much is given, much is required." We must collectively make sure that the question, "Why are Black boys Missing In Action

(MIA)?" never be asked again. People of Color and People of Concern must advocate against Black boys being MIS-EDUCATED through curriculums of genocide, INCARCERATED through the school to prison pipeline, and ANNIHILATED by police, who through implicit bias, see them as dangerous and a threat to community safety.

This admittedly, casts a dark cloud over Black boys, but together we, as a spiritual group, can reverse these negative trends by refocusing our AIM: ASSEMBLING our human and fiscal resources to create a comprehensive planning process; assessing student INFORMATION to identify academic and non-academic barriers to student progress and incorporate evidence-based strategies to produce positive outcomes; and lastly, MOBILIZING team members to implement these strategies, while tracking outcome data so that groups can monitor and improve their interventions and create a transformational model for future generations. I am convinced that we can make a difference and validate the humanity of all people—for in truth "Black Lives Matter." Peace be upon you and your sons.

Submitted in service with unconditional love,

Osceola Thomas

----

1. The Most Segregated Hour of the Week? Web.
2. Ross, Web.
3. Carlozo, Web.

Reflective Questions

1. Is the Church called to build buildings or build people? Explain.

---

2. What did Black folks do under the Civil Rights era that communities can learn from and implement today?

---

3. Why are Black boys Missing In Action (MIA) and what can we do as a community to reverse this negative trend?

Selected Bibliography

1. "10 Basic Steps in Special Education." *Center for Parent Information and Resources.* Center for Parent Information and Resources, Apr. 2014. Web. 25 June 2015.

2. "ADHD Testing Issues regarding Testing, Drugging, and Diagnosis of ADD/ADHD." *ADHD Testing Issues regarding Testing, Drugging, and Diagnosis of ADD/ADHD.* N.p., n.d. Web. 03 Mar. 2015.

3. Alexander, Michelle. "More Black Men Are In Prison Today Than Were Enslaved In 1850." N.p., 12 Oct. 2011. Web. 3 Mar. 2015.

4. Amurao, Carla. "Fact Sheet: How Bad Is the School-to-Prison Pipeline?" *PBS.* PBS, 28 Mar. 2013. Web. 25 Jan. 2015.

5. American Psychiatric Association: *Diagnostic and Statistical Manual of Mental Disorders, 5th edition.* Arlington, VA., American Psychiatric Association, 2013.

6. "Asperger Syndrome Fact Sheet." *: National Institute of Neurological Disorders and Stroke (NINDS).* N.p., 16 Apr. 2014. Web. 11 Oct. 2014.

7. Atlanta Blackstar. "You Have To See This Impressive Retort To Bill O'Reilly Telling Tavis Smiley Blacks Scare The White Power Structure." *Atlanta Blackstar.* N.p., 04 Nov. 2014. Web. 03 Jan. 2015.

8. Bhandari, Smitha, MD. "ADHD and ADD Tests: Medical Tests, Scales and Psychological Criteria." *Web*MD. 6 May 2015. Web 25 June 2015.

9. Bidwell, Allie. "How States Are Spending Money in Education." *US News*. U.S. News & World Report, 29 Jan. 2015. Web. 29 Apr. 2015.

10. Boser, Ulrich. "Teacher Diversity Revisited." *Name*. N.p., 4 May 2014. Web. 14 Feb. 2015.

11. BrainstormUSA Blog. "Obama Administration Targets "Disparate Impact" of School Discipline on Black Students." N.p., 27 Sept. 2010. Web. 02 Mar. 2015.

12. Cann, Rebecca L. "In search of Eve." *The Sciences* 27.5 (1987): 30-37.

13. Carlozo, Lou. "Black Americans Donate to Make a Difference." *Reuters*. Thomson Reuters, 23 Feb. 2012. Web. 29 Apr. 2015.

14. Criminal Justice Fact Sheet. *Criminal Justice Fact Sheet*. NAACP, n.d. Web. 06 May 2015.

15. Crum, Maddie. "The U.S. Illiteracy Rate Hasn't Changed In 10 Years." *The Huffington Post*. TheHuffingtonPost.com, 6 Sept. 2013. Web. 05 Feb. 2015.

16. Cumminos, Peter. "Race, Marriage, and Law | News | The Harvard Crimson." *Race, Marriage, and Law | News | The Harvard Crimson*. N.p., 17 Dec. 1963. Web. 03 Mar. 2015.

17. Definition of Pedagogy in English:. *Pedagogy: Definition of Pedagogy in Oxford Dictionary (American English) (US)*. N.p., n.d. Web. 03 Mar. 2015.

18. DeGrandpre, Richard, Ph.D., and Stephen P. Hinshaw, Ph.D. "Special Needs Digest.": *The Debate Continues*. N.p., 12 Feb. 2015. Web. 25 Sept. 2015.

19. Eakman, Beverly. "The Controversy Behind ADHD." *The Controversy Behind ADHD*. N.p., n.d. Web. 03 Mar. 2015.

20. "Fact Sheet: High School Diploma Options Offered In Other States." *Chemical & Engineering News* 47.10 (1969): 101A. Legislative Counsel Bureau, June 2012. Web. 3 Mar. 2015.

21. "Fast Facts." National Center For Education Statistics, n.d. Web.

22. Feierman, Lisa. "Troubling Statistics For African-American Males In The Classroom." N.p., 10 Apr. 2014. Web.

23. Fitzgerald, Terence. "The Black Prison Called." *Racismreviewcom*. N.p., 10 Jan. 2009. Web. 02 Mar. 2015.

24. Freed, Jeffrey. *Right-Brained Children in a Left-Brained World: Unlocking the Potential of Your ADD Child*. New York: Simon & Schuster, 1998.

25. "Gap Between Black and White Male High School Graduation Rates Still Widening." *Report: Gap Between Black and White Male High School Graduation Rates Still Widening | The Schott Foundation for Public Education*. The Schott Foundation for Public Education, 11 Feb. 2015. Web. 03 Mar. 2015.

26. Hing, Julianne. "Race, Disability and the School-to-Prison Pipeline - COLORLINES." *RSS*. N.p., 13 May 2014. Web. 25 Jan. 2015.

27. Hodges, Dave. "Slavery Returns to America: The Prison Industrial Complex | U. S. Politics." *Before It's News*. Before It's News, 1 Jan. 2015. Web. 07 May 2015.

28. "In Loco Parentis." *TheFreeDictionary.com*. N.p., n.d. Web. 03 Mar. 2015.

29. "Individuals With Disabilities Education Act Cost Impact On Local School Districts." *Atlas*. N.p., 3 June 2015. Web. 26 Aug. 2015.

30. "Is Public Education Failing Black Male Students?" *GOOD Magazine*. N.p., 04 Oct. 2013. Web. 26 Nov. 2014.

31. James, George G.M. "Stolen Legacy Chapter I." *Stolen Legacy: Part I: Chapter I: Greek Philosophy Is Stolen Egyptian Philosophy*. N.p., n.d. Web. 03 Mar. 2015.

32. Knafo, Saki. "1 In 3 Black Males Will Go To Prison In Their Lifetime, Report Warns." *The Huffington Post*. TheHuffingtonPost.com, 4 Oct. 2013. Web. 13 Feb. 2015.

33. Kunjufu, Jawanza. "Black Boys and Special Education – Change Is Needed!" *Find Teaching Jobs School Jobs Education Jobs at Teachersofcolorcom RSS*. N.p., 17 Apr. 2009. Web. 06 Feb. 2015.

34. Kunjufu, Jawanza. *Keeping Black Boys Out Of Special Education* (Chicago: African American Images, 2005), pp. xii

35. Lee, Trymaine. "Preschool to Prison: No Child Too Young for Zero-tolerance." *Msnbc.com*. NBC News Digital, 21 Mar. 2014. Web. 29 Apr. 2015.

36. Matheson, Kathy. "Few Teachers Are Black Men." USA Today, 9 Oct. 2009. Web.

37. Moody, Austin. "The Education for All Handicapped Children Act: A Faltering Step Towards Integration." *Educ 300 Education Reform Past and Present*. N.p., 3 May 2012. Web. 02 Mar. 2015.

38. Mulvaney, Katie. "Brown U. Student Leader: More African-American Men in Prison System Now than Were Enslaved in 1850." *@politifact*. PolitiFact, 7 Dec. 2014. Web. 07 May 2015.

39. "Parents: Get the Facts—Know Your Rights." *CCHR International*. CCHR International, 2015. Web. 25 Sept. 2015.

40. Porter, Michael. *Kill Them Before They Grow*. African American Images. Chicago, Illinois.1997.

41. Prohibition on Mandatory Medication." CCHR International, N.d., Web. 25 June 2015.

42. Qiu, Linda. "Juan Williams: No. 1 Cause of Death for African-American Males 15-34 Is Murder." *@politifact*. N.p., 24 Aug. 2014. Web. 14 Feb. 2015.

43. Rabiner, David. "New Diagnostic Criteria for ADHD - Attention Deficit Disorder Association." *New Diagnostic Criteria for ADHD - Attention Deficit Disorder Association*. N.p., n.d. Web. 03 Mar. 2015.

44. "Right to an Evaluation of a Child for Special Education Services." *Learning Disabilities Association of America*. Learning Disabilities Association of America, 16 Feb. 2013. Web. 25 June 2015.

45. Ross, Janell. "Tis the Season for Black Nonprofits to Suffer." *Tis the Season for Black Nonprofits to Suffer*. The Root, 23 Dec. 2013. Web. 29 Apr. 2015.

46. Sanchez, Claudio. "College Board 'Concerned' About Low SAT Scores." *NPR*. NPR, 26 Sept. 2013. Web. 03 Mar. 2015.

47. Sneed, Tierney. "What Youth Incarceration Costs Taxpayers." *US News*. U.S. News & World Report, 9 Dec. 2014. Web. 29 Apr. 2015.

48. "The Most Segregated Hour of the Week?" The Exchange. Christianity Today, 19 Jan. 2015. Web. 29 Apr. 2015.

49. Than, Ker. "What Is Darwin's Theory of Evolution?" *LiveScience*. TechMedia Network, 07 Dec. 2012. Web. 25 Feb. 2015.

50. "Title VI Statute." *Title VI Statute*. N.p., n.d. Web. 03 Mar. 2015.

51. Tyson, Charlie. "ACT's Annual Score Report Shows Languishing Racial Gaps, Mediocre Scores @insidehighered." *ACT's Annual Score Report Shows Languishing Racial Gaps, Mediocre Scores @ insidehighered*. N.p., 20 Aug. 2014. Web. 05 Feb. 2015.

52. "What Is Asperger's Syndrome? Symptoms, Tests, Causes, Treatments." *WebMD*. WebMD, 12 May 2013. Web. 11 Feb. 2015.

INDEX

academic ix, xi, xiii, 11, 18, 19, 21, 26, 60, 63, 74, 76, 93, 94
advocate xiii, 4, 18, 19, 29, 30, 34, 68
Asperger's 41, 45
attention deficit disorder 45
Attention Deficit Disorder 17, 43, 69, 73, 119
Attention Deficit Hyperactivity Disorder 17, 69, 73
Civil Rights 17, 113
college 10, 15, 17, 18, 20, 23, 30, 37, 45, 48, 50, 59, 61, 85, 86, 107
communities xiii, 20, 34, 35, 49, 108, 109
deficit 3, 17, 44, 45
Deficit 17, 43, 69, 73, 74, 119
differentiating 10
disenfranchised 67
disproportionate xi, 26, 30, 34
dropout 4, 62, 74, 75
education ix, xi, xii, 9, 13, 14, 16, 17, 18, 20, 27, 29, 30, 31, 33, 42, 44, 45, 47, 49, 50, 52, 53, 68, 76
Emotional Behavioral Disturbance 17
Esau 93, 94, 95
Hip Hop 65, 67, 68
Historically Black Colleges and Universities 86, 107
incarcerated 15, 47
incarceration ix, xii, xiii, 29, 31
Individuals with Disabilities 17
Isaac 94

Jacob 94, 95
Jim Crow 13, 16, 29, 52, 105
kinesthetic 46
learning disability 13, 45
learning style 10, 48, 68
learning styles 41, 42, 44
mainstream 11, 16, 17, 18, 46
medication. 53
mis-educate 26, 29
Moses 30
Nehemiah 105, 106
Parental involvement 50
pedagogy 41
People of Concern 29, 30, 53, 108
Person of Color 16, 85
Person of Concern 16, 29
public schools 25, 34, 35, 49, 62, 75
public school system xii, xiii, 17, 27, 33, 34, 41, 42, 44, 45, 47, 67, 77
public school systems 4, 16, 17, 41, 43, 46, 50, 53, 69
racism xiv, 13, 16, 25, 30, 34, 52
special education 13, 16, 20, 53
suspension 30, 61
white power structure 13, 16, 25, 27, 31, 53
wife vii

Suggested Reading List

1. *Destruction of Black Civilization* by Chancellor Williams

2. *The Mis-Education of the Negro* by Carter G. Woodson

3. *Countering the Conspiracy to Destroy Black Boys* by Jawanza Kunjufu

4. *The Willie Lynch Letter and the Making of a Slave*

5. *World's Great Men of Color* by JA Rogers

6. *The African Origin of Civilization: Myth or Reality* by Cheikh Anta Diop

7. *How Europe Underdeveloped Africa* by Walter Rodney

8. *Stolen Legacy by George* by G.M. James

9. *From Niggas to Gods* by Akil

10. *The Invisible Man* by Ralph Ellison

11. *Before the Mayflower: A History of Black America* by Lerone Bennett

12. *Nile Valley Contributions to Civilization* by Anthony T. Browder

13. *They Came Before Columbus: The African Presence in Ancient America* by Ivan Van Sertima

14. *Breaking the Psychological Chains of Slavery* by Na'im Akbar

15. *Post Traumatic Slave Syndrome by* Joy DeGruy, Ph.D.

16. *Think and Grow Rich* by Napoleon Hill

17. *Rich Dad Poor Dad* by Robert

ABOUT THE AUTHOR

Controversial Author and Public Speaker, Osceola Thomas, is a native of Trenton, New Jersey. Osceola graduated from Philadelphia Biblical University with a Bachelor of Science degree in Biblical Studies and a Master of Science degree in Church Leadership. He has spent the majority of his career fighting to keep minority youth maintained in the least restrictive environment. Currently, he and his Kimberly along with their two children, Brandon and Lauren reside in Charlotte, North Carolina.

For information on how to book Osceola for a speaking engagement, community meeting, or grant workshop, please contact his Publicist, Nicole Bond at info@thestreetscanthavemyson.com.

If this book has been a blessing to you as a parent, please take 5-minutes and do three things that will help other parents hear about The Streets Can't Have My Son.

1.) Watch and like The Streets Can't Have My Son YouTube video: https://www.youtube.com/watch?v=3ExnVsuhg18

2.) Write a review for the book on Amazon: http://www.amazon.com/Streets-Cant-Have-Son-Reversing/dp/0692383255

3.) Join a community of other parents by subscribing to The Streets Can't Have My Son movement at www.thestreetscanthavemyson.com.

Made in the USA
Las Vegas, NV
04 March 2022